LIFE AND TEACHINGS

OF V. I. LENIN

By

R. PALME DUTT

INTERNATIONAL PUBLISHERS

NEW YORK

CONTENTS

INTRODUCTION

A NUMBER of Lives of Lenin already exist in English, of varying degrees of value.

The present short and very elementary study does not attempt to repeat the ground covered by existing biographies. Its object is rather to present the significance and rôle of Lenin, not primarily as a Russian leader, but as a world leader at a critical turning-point of human history; and not primarily as a unique personality, although he was that, but as the leader and responsible representative of a world movement of direct influence and significance for us to-day.

The living ass not only kicks the dead lion, but— what is worse—patronizes him and brays over him in terms of deepest ass-nature's approval. Bourgeois hero-worshipers and reformist flunkeys of the existing order, who poured their small venom on the living Lenin, now unite to sing his praises, when they think him safely dead. Of this "canonization" of dead revolutionaries Lenin wrote in terms of burning scorn:

During the lifetime of great revolutionaries, the oppressing classes have visited relentless persecution on them and received their teaching with the most savage hostility, most furious hatred, the most ruthless campaign of lies and slanders. After their death, attempts are made to turn them into harmless icons, canonize them, and surround their *names* with a certain halo for the "consolation" of the oppressed classes and with the object of duping them, while at the same time emasculating and vulgarizing the *real essence* of their revolutionary theories and blunting their revolutionary edge.*

* V. I. Lenin, *State and Revolution* (International Publishers), p. 7.

This "canonizing" is already in full swing in relation to Lenin. The enemies of revolution, the apologists of reformism and surrender, and even the leaders of conservatism, all endeavor to praise the "realist" and "statesmanlike" qualities of Lenin, in the hope to throw the halo of his revolutionary memory over the policies of reaction and to weaken the advance of the rising revolution.

No study of Lenin can claim justification which does not strive to maintain unblunted the "revolutionary edge" of his life, work and teaching; and still more, to maintain that unity of theory and practice which was the essence of his outlook. The study of Lenin's life and work is only of value, not as an idle exercise in worship or denigration, in academic history or subjective criticism, but as a direct assistance in understanding the objective historical movement and in relation to the urgent world problems and tasks confronting us to-day.

CHAPTER I

THE EPOCH OF LENIN

LENIN was born in 1870 and died in 1924. His life thus covers the last quarter of the nineteenth century and the first quarter of the twentieth. His active life covers the last decade of the nineteenth century and the first quarter of the twentieth.

This period was a period of decisive change, a turning-point in human history. The War of 1914 and the Russian Revolution of 1917 are the outstanding signs of this turning-point, whose full meaning is only beginning to be understood. Lenin's life activity stands at the very center of this transformation.

Lenin's strength, which marks him out from all the other political thinkers and leaders of this period, was that he alone, from an early point, on the strong basis of Marxism, from well before the end of the nineteenth century, saw with complete clearness the whole character of the future period, prepared for it, drew the practical, concrete conclusions, and was alone adequate to the demands of history when the time came.

What gave Lenin this unique strength to see clearly, accurately and far into the historical movement? He drew this strength from the basis of Marxism, which he brought to new life, rescuing it from the hands of pedants, philistines and routine politicians, into whose keeping it had fallen.

In order to understand the work of Lenin it is therefore essential to understand the basis of Marxism, on which he built, and the character of the epoch in which he acted.

The essential character of Marxism is that of a single scientific world outlook on the whole of nature, life and activity.

Marxism grew up in the second quarter of the nineteenth century. At that time the basic contradictions of existing society had come already strongly to the front.

The long series of middle-class revolutions of the preceding period had established the political power of capitalism in the leading countries, especially in England, France and the United States. Capitalist relations dominated the world. Machine industry was opening up its gigantic expansion. The conceptions of liberal capitalism, which had received their ideal insurgent expression in the Rights of Man and the slogans of "Liberty, Equality and Fraternity," and then reached their consolidation in the framework of the national states, constitutional government and international trade, appeared to the new rulers, to the bourgeoisie, as the apex of human development.

But the negative side of the rule of capitalism was already appearing. For the masses of the working population the slogans of "Liberty, Equality and Fraternity" revealed themselves as an empty pretense, covering only the substitution of the rule of one class by that of another; the masses remained in conditions of grinding toil, poverty and servitude. The anarchy of production and distribution; the recurrent crises; the limitless extremes and ever-widening gulf of wealth and poverty; the wild scramble of commercialism and profit-seeking all over the world; all were revealing the inner contradictions of capitalism.

The rising new social force of the future, the working class, on whose labor the wealth of capitalism was built up, was now beginning to appear on the social-political scene as an active independent factor in gathering mass revolts, confused at first, but already showing an increas-

ing political aim and consciousness, most notably in the
early movements of revolutionary trade unionism and
Chartism in England. The bourgeoisie now turned
more and more clearly from its former revolutionary
rôle to a counter-revolutionary rôle, as the defender of
the existing order against the new forces.

Alongside the beginnings of working class revolt, the
critique of capitalism began to appear. One school
turned to medieval hankerings (Carlyle in England) or
vague humanitarian aspirations (Sismondi). Another
school endeavored to look forward to a new social
order and evolved the early theories of Utopian Socialism (St. Simon, Fourier, Owen). The Utopian Socialists criticized the evils of capitalism and advocated a
coöperative social order, but without any clear conception of social development, addressing themselves
primarily to the governing bourgeoisie who had no use
for them, and deploring the class struggle which could
alone realize their aims.

At the same time, the development of thought and
philosophy showed that the conditions were ripe for a
new stage of advance. Bourgeois thought was reaching
the limit of its development and beginning to exhaust
itself. The culmination of bourgeois classical philosophy
was reached with Hegel in the first quarter of the nineteenth century. Hegel achieved a profound revolutionary work in destroying the subjective idealisms,
dogmatic presuppositions and empirical skepticisms of
his predecessors, and establishing for the first time a
critical, objective understanding of the universe, life and
society as a systematic interconnected process of development, advancing dialectically, through contradiction
and conflict, to new forms, the laws of which process
could be understood and mastered. But he left the
ultimate factors of the process still in the mystical ideal
sphere; just as he left the state mystically outside and

above the civil society of which it was in reality the outcome and reflection. His philosophy thus still suffered
from idealism, was not completely critical and scientific,
and inevitably ended in mysticism and reaction, as a
buttress of the Prussian monarchy. Nevertheless, his
was the last great philosophical system of the bourgeoisie; after him bourgeois philosophy (apart from the
left Hegelian, Feuerbach, the materialist) passed to irrational subjectivism, empiricism, eclectic piecing together of fragments, and a good deal of charlatanry.

In the same way, the culmination of the school of
classical economists of the bourgeoisie was reached with
Ricardo in the first quarter of the nineteenth century.
The classical economists had endeavored to work out a
scientific analysis of the economic basis of the new
society. But they were tied by their unconscious presuppositions of the bourgeois order which they assumed
as a natural eternal order, and became in consequence
hopelessly entangled in the inability to discover a
scientific explanation of rent, profit and interest. Thereafter, bourgeois economics abandoned the attempt to be
a science, and confined itself to the empirical level of
market-calculations, with the consequent complete im-
potence to understand or predict major economic proc-
esses, which has made it a laughing-stock to-day.

Only the natural sciences, which were technically
useful to capitalism, were able to continue progress
through the nineteenth century, and even here only in
the face of constant conflict against the reactionary ruling forces. But the natural sciences worked only in
their separate fields, without any wider common understanding; thus leading inevitably to the subsequent
dilemmas and crises of science, when further advance
breaks down the provisional barriers and compels the
facing of a more basic understanding.

Of attempt at a scientific understanding of man's life

and history, and social and political institutions, in their total relationship, and not in isolation, there was hardly even the conception before Marx.

Thus, humanity before Marxism developed *blindly,* through the blind interplay of opposing forces, often with terrible results, without attempt at collective understanding.

This blind development still continues, as far as the old forces are dominant (the World War, the present world economic crisis) ; but the new organizing force of collective scientific understanding and action (Marxism or international Communism, represented by the international working class) is able to play an increasingly powerful rôle at every stage, and will ultimately control the process.

It was at this critical stage of the nineteenth century, when new forces, problems and conflicts were growing up on every side, while the power of the ruling bourgeois thought to deal with them was weakening and drying up, that Marx, building on a profound study of all previous thought and knowledge, and of existing world realities, was able to break through the obstacles and show the way forward, and thus stands out in the nineteenth century as the maker and builder of the modern world.

Marx first worked out a fully scientific world outlook and method. This is the outlook of dialectical materialism.

Marx built on the dialectic of Hegel, but freed it from its arbitrary idealist elements. With Feuerbach, the materialist disciple of Hegel, he saw that the ideal world was no mystical creation out of nothing, but the reflection of the material world. But he differed from the passive materialism of Feuerbach, or the mechanical materialism of the French and English materialists, in that he brought out the practical rôle of the thought-process and human activity, not merely as the passive reflection of the material world, but as in turn acting upon and transforming the material world. Hence, the distinctive character of dialectical materialism, in its unity of theory and practice. "Philosophers have only explained the world in different ways; the task is to change it" (Karl Marx, "Theses on Feuerbach"). This conception reaches its full realization in the lives of both Marx and Lenin.

On the basis of this outlook, Marx was able to analyze the development of human history, no longer as an irrational jumble of accidents, nor as the fulfillment of arbitrary ideas and notions, but as a systematic scientifically explicable development, based on the given stage of the material forces of production and consequent necessary forms of social relationship, giving rise to corresponding forms of social consciousness, class relations, ideology, social and political structure, and consequent conflicts and contradictions, leading to further development.

The whole of recorded past history—subsequent to the period of primitive communism when the low level of production and absence of surplus left no scope for class division and exploitation—thus becomes revealed as a succession of different forms of class society and class domination, corresponding to different stages of production, and developing through a series of class struggles.

Capitalism is seen on this outlook, not as a permanent inevitable "natural necessity" or super-historical "economic law" (as the bourgeois professors tried to make believe), but as a historical phase, with a beginning and with an end—the last phase of class society. Capitalism, growing out of the conditions of feudalism and small-property society, replaces, or thrusts to the background, the previous dominant forms of class privilege and division by a new form—the division of the bourgeoisie or property-owning class who live by the employment of others' labor, and the proletariat or dispossessed wage-earning class, who are nominally free, but are in fact dependent for their livelihood on the bourgeoisie. The discovery of the laws of motion of capitalist society was the specific work of Marx in applying the methods of dialectical materialism to the existing stage of social development. He was able to show that capitalism in its early stages, despite wholesale cruelty and hardship, was nevertheless a progressive force, driving through competition to continual development of the productive forces, enlargement of the scale of production, concentration of capital and increasing of the numbers of the proletariat. But by this very process capitalism prepares its own destruction. Originating on a basis of individual property ownership, capitalism develops to the opposite, to a gigantic, though anarchic, large-scale organization of production, in which the overwhelming mass of producers are cut off from ownership, while the appropriation of the fruits by the small and increasingly parasitic owning class becomes a fetter on the further development of production. The conditions are thus ripe for the next stage. Capitalism becomes a reactionary, and no longer a progressive, force. The growing contradictions and approaching downfall of capitalism are heralded in the successively greater choking of the machine, enlarging crises and periods of stagnation, mass poverty in the midst of colossal wealth and wealth-producing power, and the rising conflicts of the bourgeoisie and the proletariat. The proletariat is compelled by the conditions of its existence to organize collectively and seek salvation in the common ownership of the means of production. The class struggle of the proletariat becomes the sole progressive force, requiring to be carried forward

to the revolutionary point when the proletariat con-
quers political power, takes over the means of production from the capitalists and organizes social production
for use, thus inaugurating the classless society. In this
outcome Marx found the solution for the problems of
the present epoch.

The central task of our epoch Marx thus sees as the
realization of the dictatorship of the proletariat to
organize production socially and lead the way to the
classless communist society of the future.

This task requires the international revolutionary
organization of the proletariat to accomplish its world
mission.

To this task Marx and his co-worker, Engels, who
shares with him the honor both of the original elabora-
tion of the theory and of the leadership of the practical
fight, devoted their lives, both on the theoretical and
on the practical front.

In the growth and shaping of the international working class movement through the second half of the
nineteenth century Marx and Engels played the leading
part. Through the international Communist League,
through the First International, and through direct
contact with the working-class movements of the different countries throughout the world, Marx and Engels
trained and guided the rising international working-
class movement. By the death of Marx in 1883, and
still more by the time of the death of Engels, in 1895,
Marxism was the recognized basis of the entire international working-class movement.

But the decisive battle of capitalism and the proletarian revolution was not to come until after the deaths of
Marx and Engels. Although the revolutionary struggles of 1848, and still more the Paris Commune of 1871,
when the workers held power for six weeks, showed the
way forward, capitalism had still before it a period of

expansion of its range throughout the world before it reached the era of decay, and before the period of the world revolution could open.

The world expansion of capitalism led to a stage in which the greater part of the world became directly subjected to the handful of capitalist powers of Europe and the United States. The partition of the world reached completion in its main lines by the last quarter of the nineteenth century. The monopoly capitalism of the Western Powers held the world in tribute. Enormous profits flowed to the ruling financial class; a portion of these were used to buy off the rising labor movements by the concession of limited reforms and by the corruption of the leadership. Capitalism entered into the stage of decline and parasitism, leading to the World War and the present general crisis—the stage of imperialism or, as Lenin defined it, the last stage of capitalism.

The epoch of imperialism was the epoch of Lenin.

Marx and Engels did not live to witness more than the barest opening of the epoch of imperialism, to the character of which their writings had already given the clew.

The leadership of international socialism passed from Marx and Engels to Lenin. It passed, in fact, to Lenin throughout this epoch, although it was not internationally recognized and effective until the victory of 1917 proved its claims.

In the first stages of imperialism, after the deaths of Marx and Engels, a wave of confusion and weakening of the revolutionary aim passed over the international working-class movement. The great mass organizations of the Socialist parties and the trade unions, organized in the Second International since 1889 and in the International Federation of Trade Unions, grew enormously in numbers and strength. The Socialist International numbered twelve millions by 1914. The program of Marxism remained in name the program. But the practice turned increasingly to opportunism, that is, to adaptation to the existing capitalist régime for the sake of limited immediate concessions.

The true character of the period of imperialism was not at first understood even by many Socialists. A whole theory of opportunism grew up within the ranks of international socialism. This theory regarded the period of imperialism as a refutation of the teachings of Marx: as an advance of capitalism to new life and higher organization, overcoming its conflicts; as a period of the gradual reconciliation of contradictions, of social reform and increasing improvement of conditions for all, and of the peaceful advance to socialism. These theories were in principle refuted and condemned by the Socialist International; nevertheless, they increasingly dominated in practice.

The World War dealt the death-blow to these illusions, revealing the real character of imperialism as a period of violent crises and explosions, of ever-widening mass misery, and of the advance to the proletarian revolution.

The greater part of Lenin's life, two-thirds of his active political life, was spent in the pre-War imperialist epoch, in the midst of the deepening slough of opportunism and denial of revolution within the ranks of international socialism. In the battle for revolutionary Marxism against opportunism Lenin grew up and grew strong, and steeled the party that he led for the coming conflicts.

The World War brought the crisis and downfall of the old Socialist International. The supreme crisis and violent bursting of all the contradictions, to which Marx had long before pointed, brought the supreme test of international socialism. The old Socialist International, soaked in opportunism, broke down at the test. It broke asunder, and its leading parties passed openly to the service of the various warring imperialisms.

This moment was the blackest moment in modern history. The fate of humanity, to escape from the bog of destruction into which imperialism was bringing it, was bound up with international socialism. The moment which had been long foreseen and prepared for had come; the instrument, which had been built up with the labor and sacrifice of generations to be ready for the crisis was at hand; and the instrument appeared to have failed. It looked as if the whole labor would have to begin again from the foundations at the twelfth hour, in a now desperate race against the forces of destruction.

Nevertheless, international socialism had not failed. The forces that were to carry forward the movement, to be equal to the demands of the crisis, and to open the victorious world revolution, were there. The center of these forces was Lenin.

Marx died in 1883. Engels died in 1895.

By 1893 Lenin had entered on his leading political activity, to be continued without a break until his last illness in 1923.

CHAPTER II

THE LIFE OF LENIN

THE NAME of Lenin is already the first indication as to the character of his life and work. The birth-name of Lenin was Vladimir Ilyitch Ulyanov. He was born at Simbirsk (now renamed Ulyanovsk) in Russia (now the Union of Socialist Soviet Republics) on April 22, 1870. The name of Lenin, by which the whole world knows him, was originally a revolutionary pseudonym, adopted only after manhood to meet the needs of illegal revolutionary work under tsarism.

Such conditions of illegal revolutionary work were almost unknown at the time in most of the rest of Europe, save for the very much milder example of the Anti-Socialist Laws of Bismarck in Germany during the 'eighties. They were considered essentially peculiar to the "backwardness" of Russia. To-day the tables are turned. Over the great part of Europe such methods of illegal revolutionary work are becoming obligatory for conducting, not only the most elementary socialist propaganda, but even the most elementary political fight against complete servitude. The "backwardness" of tsarism held in fact the mirror, in many respects, to the future of the European nations in the period of imperialist decay; the revolutionary movement which grew up under those conditions has become the strongest and most advanced; while in the "advanced" European countries the movements which had prided themselves on their strength and leading rôle are now painfully compelled to learn the methods of struggle under the whip of the counter-revolution. This pro-

found historical transposition is of the greatest importance for understanding the rôle of the Russian revolutionary working-class movement, led by Lenin, in the
international sphere.

1. THE BASIC CONCEPTIONS AND FOUNDATIONS OF LENIN'S WORK

The legend is sometimes given currency that Lenin
was completely unknown in world politics, or known
only to a small band of faithful disciples, before 1917.
Thus one of the most recent romantic biographies in
English declares that "it is not an overstatement to say
that he was an unknown person in the public life of
the world until October, 1917."

This is not correct. Apart from his leadership in
the old Socialist International, on whose bureau he
played for a period an active part, his historical rôle was
familiar even to bourgeois observers outside Russia
already before the War. Thus a standard work such as
the *Cambridge Modern History,* published in 1910, in a
short chapter on the preceding half century of Russian
history devotes half a page to the work and theories of
Lenin as one of the significant influences of the last
decade of the nineteenth century and first decade of the
twentieth in Russia.*

The victory of the Bolshevik Revolution in 1917 was,
in fact, no miraculous explosion suddenly blazing out as
if from nothing, but the culmination of the long previous process of the revolutionary movement in Russia
within which the thirty years' tireless preparatory work
of Lenin played a decisive part.

Lenin has himself written, after the revolution, how
Bolshevism or revolutionary Marxism in Russia was the
outcome of the entire preceding revolutionary development:

* *Cambridge Modern History,* 1910 edition, Vol. XII, pp. 331-2.

For half a century, approximately between the 'forties and the 'nineties of the preceding century, advanced intellects in Russia under the yoke of the most savage and reactionary tsarism, sought eagerly the correct revolutionary theory, following the "last word" in Europe and America with astounding diligence and thoroughness, in order to find it.

Russia has attained Marxism, the only revolutionary theory, by dint of fifty years travail and sacrifice, through the greatest revolutionary heroism, the most incredible energy, by unselfish pursuit, training, education, practical tests, disappointments, checking up and comparison with European experience. Thanks to the emigration forced by the Tsar, revolutionary Russia, in the second half of the nineteenth century, acquired rich international connections, and an excellent grasp of the forms and theories of the revolutionary movement such as no other country had.*

This unique character of the revolutionary movement in Russia, its long training in practical revolutionary work, in revolutionary sacrifice and heroism, its profound theoretical character, and its unrivaled international background is essential to grasp in order to understand how the ground was prepared for the development of strong, undistorted and victorious revolutionary Marxism in Russia before all other countries.

Despite the late appearance of the industrial proletariat in Russia, the ground was from the first more fully prepared in many respects for advance than elsewhere. The first translation of Marx's *Capital* into any language appeared in Russia in 1872, five years after the original issue of the work, in an edition of 3,000, which was almost at once sold out. The first French translation appeared in 1883, the first English in 1886, or fourteen years after the Russian.

The first Russian Marxist organization was that of the "Liberation of Labor," founded in emigration by Plek-

* V. I. Lenin, *"Left-Wing" Communism, an Infantile Disorder* (International Publishers).

hanov and others in 1883. Its second program, issued
in 1887, provided the foundation for the program of
Social-Democracy in Russia.

In 1887 Lenin, then aged seventeen, was expelled
from Kazan University, which he had just entered as a
student, for participation in a revolutionary demonstration. Earlier in the same year, his elder brother, Alexander, had been hanged for planning an attempt on
the Tsar. These were Lenin's early direct experience
of the revolutionary movement.

The father of Lenin was an inspector of schools. The
two sons and four daughters all studied deeply, and
were all revolutionaries. Alexander, the eldest, was the
last leading representative of the old pre-Marxist revolutionary organization, the *Narodnaya Volya* or People's
Will, which sought to overthrow tsarism by individual
terrorism. Lenin honored deeply the memory of his
brother and of the old revolutionary fighters of the
Narodniki, who had bequeathed a heroic tradition.
But he saw that these methods did not avail to overthrow tsarism. He sought earnestly the answer to the
problems of the struggle for liberation. He found the
answer in Marxism. From Marx he learnt the scientific
approach to the laws of social development; that the
power of the existing régime could only be overthrown,
not by individual action, but by mass action, and that
the leader of the future victorious revolution must be
the industrial working class. Lenin studied Marx's
writings with extreme thoroughness, so far as it was
possible to get hold of them under the conditions of very
great difficulty. At the same time he continued his
studies, and took his degree in law at Petersburg in
1891. For over a year he worked as assistant to a law-
yer at Samara. Both at Kazan and at Samara he took
part in Marxist circles, the first forms of Social-Democratic groups before any party existed. He wrote his

first work in 1893, bearing on the peasant question. In the autumn of 1893 he came to Petersburg. From then his leading political activity began.

The first task was to clear the political line of Social-Democracy and to begin the organization of the workers on the line of Social-Democracy, with a view to the formation of a Social-Democratic Party. This task was accomplished in the years 1894-8.

A great confusion of outlooks and tendencies existed at the time in the field of revolutionary and semi-revolutionary thought and activity of a socialistic type. On the other hand, there were the Narodniki or surviving representatives of the pre-Marxist movement (their outlook later passed to the Socialist-Revolutionary Party) who idealized the peasantry, denied the necessity of the development of capitalism and machine industry in Russia, and saw in the village commune the basis for socialism. Against them were ranged the Marxist. But among the Marxists were many of a professorial or non-revolutionary legalist type (legal Marxism), who embraced the economic analysis of Marxism to fight the sentimental idealist anti-capitalist conceptions, but in practice tended to draw back from the revolutionary organization of the workers and subordinate the workers to capitalism, and thus became in reality propagandists of capitalism, as the subsequent evolution of their leaders (Struve, Tugan-Baranovsky) to liberalism revealed. Finally, there were the revolutionary Marxists, of whom Lenin rapidly after his arrival in Petersburg became the effective leader, with Plekhanov as the leader in emigration.

From the outset Lenin laid down with absolute clearness the line of revolutionary social-democracy and marked it off from the opposing tendencies. This he accomplished already in 1894.

By the issue (illegally) of his first important work, in

1894, *Who are the Friends of the People and How do they fight the Social-Democrats?*, Lenin closed accounts with the Narodniki, and laid down the political line of social-democracy in Russia. He showed on the basis of facts the course of economic development; he showed the rôle of the working class as the future leader of the revolution for the overthrow of absolutism and the victory of socialism; and he showed the next steps that were necessary for the building of a Social-Democratic Party.

Alongside this, on the other front, in 1894, he opened fire on legal Marxism by his *Economic Content of Narodnik Theory and its Criticism in Mr. Struve's Book,* and showed that legal Marxism leads to the camp of the bourgeoisie.

This fight on two fronts, the clear demarcation of the line of revolutionary social-democracy from opposing tendencies, and at the same time concrete explanation of practical tasks, was characteristic of Lenin's leadership from the outset.

At the same time Lenin and the group of revolutionary Marxists organized groups of workers from the Petersburg factories. The distinctive character of their work was that they combined agitation and organization of the workers on the basis of their immediate conditions and the first elementary forms of class struggle with training the workers in political understanding, in the principles of Marxism, and in the consciousness of their political rôle as the future leaders of the revolution. This union of politics and the masses, of the revolutionary political struggle and of the daily class struggle, was from first to last one of the secrets of Bolshevism and of its strength.

In 1895 Lenin and his group were able to form the Union for the Struggle and Emancipation of the Working Class, the precursor of the Social-Democratic Party.

The Union was able to lead the rising strike movement in Petersburg. In the same year, 1895, Lenin, after a visit to Plekhanov in Switzerland (who recognized in Lenin the future leader of the Russian Revolution), was preparing to issue an illegal worker's newspaper, the *Workers' Cause,* to hold together and guide the rising movement. But on the eve of its issue he was arrested, and after a year's imprisonment, exiled for three years to Siberia till 1900. He continued his work under these conditions, assisting in the leadership of the strike movement from prison in Petersburg, and writing in Petersburg and in exile, among other things, *The Development of Capitalism in Russia,* which became and remains a classic work. He was joined in Siberia in exile by Krupskaya, who had been one of the leading members of the revolutionary Marxist group in Petersburg; they continued their common life and work without a break until Lenin's death.

By 1898 the Russian Social-Democratic Labor Party was formed at a first congress in Minsk; but Lenin in exile was not able to take part. The *Manifesto* of the Congress was in fact drafted by the leader of legal Marxism, Struve.

A period of confusion and weakness of direction in the young social-democracy followed. The old guard of the leaders of revolutionary Marxism around Lenin of 1894-8 were all in prison or exile. Those who came now to the front fell under the influence of opportunist ideas, especially emanating from western social-democracy. It was at this time (1899) that Bernstein issued his book which began the campaign of revisionist social-ism against revolutionary Marxism, and opened an international battle in the name of "freedom of criticism" (in reality, passing over to bourgeois ideas) against "orthodoxy" (Marxism). At the same time, opportunism took on a distinctive character in Russia in the

theory and practice which became known as Economism, reflecting certain western models. The advocates
of this tendency argued that "politics" were above the
heads of the workers; that Social-Democrats should
concentrate on leading and organizing the workers on
the basis of their immediate practical interests in the
daily economic struggle against the employers, as in
British trade unionism; and that from this economic
struggle would later develop political consciousness and
the political struggle. This conception meant, in fact,
leaving the political field to the bourgeoisie; it meant,
as the example of British trade unionism showed, servitude to the bourgeoisie.

Lenin at once opened merciless war on these opportunist tendencies which were endangering the whole
future of the Russian working-class movement, and
would have produced only servile laborism in place of
revolutionary social-democracy. As soon as he was back
in Russia, he began a series of articles, which finally
reached completed form in the book *What Is To Be
Done?* published in 1902.* In this book the distinctive
contribution of Bolshevism to the working-class movement first appears, fully armed; and its contents remain
of vital importance to the international working-class
movement to-day.

The essence of *What Is To Be Done?* is the demonstration of the leading political rôle of revolutionary
social-democracy, and the exposure of the false, supposedly "Marxist theory" of the "spontaneous" development of the class struggle of the workers to socialist
consciousness and revolution. The spontaneous class
struggle of the workers against the capitalists does not
yet lead to socialist consciousness, but only to trade
union consciousness, which remains subordinate to capitalist ideas. Marxism, or socialist consciousness, requires

* V. I. Lenin, *What Is To Be Done?* (International Publishers).

complete scientific knowledge of social laws and the conditions of social transformation; this does not arise naturally for the workers, who are cut off from knowledge; it must be taught. Socialist consciousness, the revolutionary consciousness of the workers of their historic rôle, not merely as a special section in society fighting for their limited immediate interests, but as the leaders of social transformation, as the leaders of the struggle of all the oppressed, the destroyers of the old society and the builders of a new society; this consciousness must be awakened in the workers by the active leadership of social-democracy. This is the task of social-democracy. Social-democrats must not therefore be satisfied with confining themselves to special, limited, narrow, supposedly "working-class" interests; their agitation and leadership must range over every political issue, must raise the fight against the existing order at every point. To accomplish these tasks, the old, loose, amateurish forms of organization and methods of work are useless; in the conflict with the modern state machine, they are like primitive handicrafts pitted against large-scale machine industry. Social-democracy must be organized as a disciplined, centralized party based on democratic centralism, and led by professional revolutionaries, trained and capable of conducting the fight against the existing order at every point and through every stage of the struggle.

These conceptions, expressed with all the explosive power of original and genuinely revolutionary thought, carrying forward Marxism realistically to all the problems of the existing struggle, burst like a bombshell through Russian social-democracy. On these conceptions the Bolshevik Party led by Lenin was built up, and the revolutionary working-class movement in Russia was trained. The result is visible to-day. The Russian working class was able to rise to the stature of its revolutionary mission, and to-day rules its country and builds a new society. The western European and American working class, despite the longer development of their movement, remains so far in bondage.

2. BOLSHEVISM AND MENSHEVISM

The political life of Lenin reveals one long fight for the line of revolutionary Marxism against opportunism (and, when necessary, against its twin brother, empty phrase-making "leftism"). From the beginning of his leading activity in 1894 to the victory of the Revolution in 1917 he was conducting ceaselessly this indispensable inner fight within social-democracy, on the fate of which depended the future of the Russian working class. He conducted this fight fearlessly and mercilessly, never hesitating to make a break when he was convinced that this was indispensable in order to build a revolutionary mass party. His fight was understood at the time by few outside his supporters. The majority of the leaders of international socialism accused him of incurable sectarianism, doctrinairism, quarreling over phrases, fractionalism, etc., and repeatedly offered their good offices to "reconcile" and "unite" the warring sections—offers which were politely, but firmly, refused. It was a difficult path that Lenin chose; but he knew what he was doing, and that his line had nothing in common with sectarianism and doctrinairism, but reflected real understanding of the needs of a revolutionary mass party. The event has proved his justification. To-day the Bolshevik Party that he built up with such minute and combative attention to every detail of program, tactics and organization, is the largest mass party in the world.

The central form in which these differences crystallized and in which they have become well known throughout the world, was the form of Bolshevism and Menshevism. The division of Bolshevism and Menshevism dates from the Second Congress of the Russian Social-Democratic Labor Party in 1903, although the issue was already showing itself in preliminary forms in the fight against Economism and against legal Marxism.

How did the division arise? One of the main conceptions of Lenin, elaborated in *What Is To Be Done?* was the issuing of a central newspaper, as a "collective agitator and organizer," which would bind together the scattered groups and help to build up the centralized party. To this task Lenin set himself on his return from exile. By a decision of a conference of revolutionary Social-Democrats at Pskov, the three outstanding leaders in Russia, Lenin, Martov and Potressov, were mandated to go abroad to join the group of older leaders in emigration, Plekhanov, Axelrod and Vera Zasulitch, for the issuing of a central organ. This aim was realized by the publication from abroad of the *Iskra (Spark)* in 1900. From 1900 to 1903 the *Iskra* built up the party and its political line. On the basis of its work and connections it was possible to call a representative Congress in 1903, numbering forty-four delegates, of whom four were workers, from twenty-six organizations. This Congress met first in Brussels, and then, driven from there by the police, in London.

At this congress the supporters of the *Iskra* overwhelmingly outnumbered the reactionary forces of the Economists and of the Jewish Bund (who were unwilling to enter a single centralized party). But a division appeared among the supporters of the *Iskra*. It is this division that developed to Bolshevism and Menshevism. The Bolsheviks, led by Lenin, at first together with Plekhanov, won the majority in the election of the Central Commitee and of the Editorial Board; hence they became known as "the majority men" (Bolsheviks) ; the Mensheviks, led by Martov, were the minority. In point of fact, the division was close. On one of the principal issues, that of the Party Statute, the Mensheviks won. And almost immediately after the Congress Plekhanov joined the Mensheviks. Lenin was left in complete isolation in the leadership, had to resign from the *Iskra,* to begin a new journal, the *Vperiod (Forward),* and to organize "Bureaux of the Majority" in Russia to maintain the Bolshevik organization. Through these in the beginning of 1905 the Third Congress was organized and held in London. The Third Congress was a fully Bolshevik Congress, and laid down for the first time with complete clearness through all its decisions the lines of Bolshevik tactics.

What were the issues which divided the Bolsheviks and Mensheviks? The division developed on a number of issues, especially:

1. The conception of the revolution. Since the immediate task of the future revolution was the overthrow of tsarism and feudalism, that is, the fulfillment of the bourgeois-democratic revolution already completed in western Europe, the Mensheviks held that the régime and government succeeding tsarism must necessarily be that of the bourgeoisie, and that the rôle of the working class would be to strive to win concessions within this régime, while giving it general support. The Bolsheviks argued that the revolution could only conquer, not under the leadership of the bourgeoisie, but under the leadership of the working class, in alliance with the peasantry; and that the working class must fight to establish the revolutionary democratic dictatorship of the workers and peasants as the form of state to succeed tsarism.

2. The relationship to the liberal bourgeoisie. The Mensheviks favored alliance with the liberal bour-

geoisie, on condition of the latter promising to support the workers' demands. The Bolsheviks, while ready to utilize all tactics according to circumstances, insisted on the necessity to expose uncompromisingly the real character of the aims and reactionary rôle of the liberal bourgeoisie.

3. The conception of the party. The Mensheviks favored a more elastic form of party organization, which would leave membership open to individual supporters of the program (isolated intellectuals, etc.) who were not directly members of the underground working groups, but only worked under their control; that is, in effect, to sympathizers who hesitated to face the consequences of direct revolutionary work. The Bolsheviks insisted that the party would only be the weaker for these elements, and must consist solely of members directly participating as responsible party workers in a party organization; only on this basis could the party be an effective revolutionary, disciplined, fighting force, without weak, passive or vacillating elements.

These were some of the principal issues dividing Bolshevism and Menshevism in the early years. It will be seen that these issues already contained in germ the essential line of division between revolutionary socialism and reformism, between the fight for the workers' revolution and the line of adaptation to capitalism. This division revealed its true character more and more completely in the succeeding years. Menshevism developed to the line of "national defense" or support of imperialism during the War; to ministerial coalition with the bourgeoisie after the revolution in March, 1917, maintaining imperialism and throwing the Bolsheviks into prison; and finally to armed counter-revolution after the Bolshevik capture of power, when the Mensheviks joined the White camp of the bourgeois and monarchist forces in open war on the workers' rule.

This subsequent working out, step by step, of the whole character of Menshevism, which was in fact no peculiar Russian phenomenon, but is an international tendency, proved the correctness of Lenin's judgment of its character at the outset.

The first Russian Revolution of 1905 brought all the questions of theory and tactics to the test of practice, and laid bare the future lines of 1917. Here was demonstrated the power of the mass struggle of the workers and peasants as the force shaking tsarism and bringing it to its knees; the rôle of the class-conscious workers and their party organization as the leader in the fight; and the hesitating and finally counter-revolutionary rôle of the liberal bourgeoisie passing over at the critical moment to compromise with tsarism. A flood of light was thrown on the rôle of the strike movement, developing to the political general strike, and to the armed rising; this new experience of the forms and methods of struggle aroused passionate controversy and a new militant awakening throughout international social-democracy. The foremost theorists of international social-democracy, such as Kautsky, who then still fought for the principles of revolutionary Marxism, recognized at that time the leadership of the international socialist revolution was passing to the Russian proletariat. The first Soviets, or Councils of Workers' Delegates, the future organs of the workers' power, grew up in the struggle of 1905 in Petersburg, Moscow and other centers.

The opposing tactics of Bolshevism and Menshevism were further demonstrated in the 1905 Revolution. The Mensheviks saw the task of the workers' struggle to exert pressure on and drive forward the bourgeoisie as the leadership of the revolution. But the Bolsheviks sought to press forward the independent leading rôle

of the proletariat, developed the political character of
the strike movement, worked out a new agrarian program to draw the peasants' struggle for land into the
general political struggle by the organization of peasants' committees to divide the land, and carried forward
the mass struggle to the highest point in the December
armed rising in Moscow, which was initiated under the
auspices of the Moscow Soviet and led by the Bolsheviks, and which held the Tsar's troops for ten days.
The Mensheviks deplored the armed rising, which was
crushed in blood, as inopportune and a mistake. Lenin
criticized the errors in tactics which were made, but
saw in the armed rising "the greatest historical achievement of the Russian Revolution" and the signpost to
future victory.

. . . Nothing could be more short-sighted than Plekhanov's view, which is adopted by all the opportunists, that
the strike was inopportune and should not have been
started and that they "should not have taken up arms." On
the contrary, they should have taken to arms more reso-
lutely, energetically and aggressively, it should have been
explained to the masses that peaceful strikes by themselves
were useless, and that fearless and ruthless armed fighting
was required. . . . To conceal from the masses the necessity
for a desperate, sanguinary, exterminating war as the immediate task of future revolutionary action—means to deceive
both ourselves and the people.*

Tsarism was for the moment victorious. The finance-
capital of "democratic" Britain and France came to the
rescue of reactionary tsarism, and bolstered it up with
enormous loans, without which it would have undoubt-
edly fallen. Bloody reaction set in. Lenin, who had
returned to Russia in 1905 to lead the struggle on the
spot, from the conditions of illegality, had to return to
emigration in 1907.

* V. I. Lenin, "The Lessons of the Moscow Uprising," in *The Revolution of 1905* (Little Lenin Library, Vol. 6), pp. 30-36.

During the period of reaction different tactics had to be pursued, of patient, persistent mass work, utilizing every smallest possibility. Many lost heart and dropped out. The Bolsheviks had lost most heavily in sacrifices, both of those killed and of those imprisoned. In the period of reaction the Mensheviks came to the front; they declared that there was no longer scope for revolutionary activity, that it was necessary to "liquidate" the illegal revolutionary party, and concentrate instead on building legal trade unions and a legal workers' party, with a limited program of immediate demands for concessions. At the same time Lenin had to combat "left" passive sectarian tendencies among some of the Bolsheviks (Otsovism, as this tendency was called), who proposed to boycott the reactionary Third Duma, thus showing that they did not understand the necessity in a period of reaction to utilize every smallest legal possibility alongside illegal work. Others again became lost in philosophical speculation, following the latest fashionable tendencies of bourgeois thought, and seeking to "correct" the "antiquated" notions of Marx and Engels in the light of these, although in reality only falling into the oldest bourgeois fallacies. Lenin, in the midst of the tasks of political leadership, saw the danger also of these tendencies, and dealt fully with the philosophical questions raised in his book, *Materialism and Empirio-Criticism* * (1908), which remains the indispensable guide for assisting all to-day who wish to understand the outlook of dialectical materialism.

The leadership of Lenin in the years of reaction 1907-1911, and the combined fight against "liquidationist" and Otsovist tendencies, is no less instructive than the early years of building the party or the correct fight of the 1905 Revolution. During these years, Bolshevism,

* V. I. Lenin, *Materialism and Empirio-Criticism* (Collected Works, Vol. XIII, International Publishers).

in place of being wiped out by the reaction, became deeply rooted in the working class and established itself as the leader of the majority of the industrial workers. The leader of Menshevism, T. Dan, had later to write of this period in the official party history of Menshevism:

Whilst the Bolshevik section of the party transformed itself into a battle-phalanx, held together by iron discipline and cohesive guiding resolution, the ranks of the Menshevik section were ever more seriously disorganized by dissension and apathy.*

The fruits of this tenacious fight and mass work were revealed when a new rising wave of struggle began in 1911 with the Bolsheviks in indisputable leadership. The split of the Bolsheviks and Mensheviks was now completed into two parties, with the Bolshevik Congress of January, 1912. The Mensheviks had seven deputies in the Duma, from non-proletarian districts with only 214,000 workers. All the industrial districts, with a total of 1,008,000 workers, returned Bolshevik deputies, numbering six. The measure of the workers' subscriptions to the Bolshevik daily, *Pravda,* begun in 1912, in contrast to those to the Menshevik organ (in effect, the only legal and controllable measure of relative membership) showed the same picture: the Bolsheviks by 1914 united eighty per cent of the class-conscious workers, the Mensheviks only twenty per cent.

From 1912 to 1914 Lenin led the growing fight from close to the Russian border, in Galicia. On the eve of the War in 1914 the signs of revolution were close; a widespread strike movement was culminating in barricades in the streets of Petersburg. The imperialist war was able for the moment to turn back the steam, only to give it enormously greater force when it returned in 1917.

---

* T. Dan, "Social Democracy in Russia after 1908"; Appendix to Martov's *History of Russian Social-Democracy,* Berlin, 1926.

3. THE WORLD WAR AND REVOLUTIONARY INTERNATIONALISM

The World War of 1914-1918 was the turning point which showed that capitalism had entered into the period of violent crisis and break-up, and that the hour had sounded for the world socialist revolution to begin.

The world socialist revolution began in 1917 at the weakest point in the chain of imperialism, Russia, and under the leadership of the most advanced and strongest revolutionary socialist party, the Bolshevik Party, led by Lenin.

This was the center point and turning point in Lenin's life, and the center point and turning point in modern history.

The Socialist International in its resolutions had long clearly foreseen this approaching crisis of war, and its significance as the starting point of revolution, and had explicitly laid down in binding and unanimous decisions the duty of all Socialist parties in this situation. The resolution of the International Socialist Congress at Stuttgart in 1907, repeated at Copenhagen in 1910, and at Basle in 1912, declared:

If war threatens to break out, it is the duty of the working class in the countries concerned, and of their parliamentary representatives, supported by the coördinating activity of the International Socialist Bureau, to exert every effort to prevent the outbreak of war by all the means which seem to them most appropriate, having regard to the sharpness of the class war and of the general political situation.

Should war none the less break out, their duty is to intervene to bring it promptly to an end, and with all their energies to strive to utilize the economic and political crisis created by the war in order to arouse the masses and thereby to hasten the overthrow of capitalist class rule.

The Basle resolution of 1912 further strengthened this declaration by direct references to the Commune as the outcome of the Franco-Prussian War, and to the First Russian Revolution as the outcome of the Russo-Japanese War.

This most important decision of the old pre-War International, the above-quoted explicit declaration of the task of Socialists in the event of war, which became the guiding line of all revolutionary Socialists during the War, had, in fact, been drafted by Lenin and Rosa Luxemburg and submitted by the latter, as mandated representative of the Russian Bolshevik Party, originally as an amendment to the resolution on war. It was unanimously adopted by all parties, including the British Labor Party. Through this decision Lenin was already, through the forms of the old Second International, exercising his leadership throughout the ranks of international socialism in every country in the world, when the crisis came, although many who were following his lead did not yet know his name or the authorship of the lead they were following.

When the test of war came in 1914, and the need to translate the resolution into action, the Second International collapsed. The majority of the Socialist parties of the leading countries were rotten with opportunism, legalism and adaptation to the capitalist régime; their leadership had long ceased in practice to be revolutionary. The War brought this into the open. The leadership of the British, French, German, Belgian and Austrian parties passed over openly to the side of the imperialist governments, voted the war credits, called on the workers to slaughter one another, and entered into coalition war governments. Only the Russian and Serbian parties stood by the line of international socialism and carried out their pledges without flinching. The Bolshevik deputies in the Duma voted against the war credits and were deported to Siberia. In December, 1914, Liebknecht voted against the war credits in Germany. The Bolsheviks and the Liebknecht-Luxemburg group in Germany became the leadership for the rebuilding of international socialism.

Lenin was the first and only leader of international socialism to face at the outset the full consequences of this collapse and to draw the practical conclusions of the line to follow. At the outbreak of the War he was in Austria, and was thrown in prison by the Austrian Government. Liberated after a fortnight, he made his way to Switzerland, and from there carried on his agitation until the Revolution in Russia in 1917. By the beginning of September, 1914, he had written his theses on the "Tasks of Revolutionary Social-Democracy in the European War," * which already contained his complete line. These were adopted by the Bolsheviks abroad and in Russia, and were developed into the *Manifesto* of the Central Committee of the Russian Social-Democratic Labor Party,** written by Lenin in October, and published on November 1, 1914. The September theses were discussed and partly adopted by the Italo-Swiss Socialist Conference at Lugano in September, 1914, which was the forerunner of the Zimmerwald International Socialist Conference in September, 1915. At Zimmerwald the revolutionary left-wing was led by Lenin, and gained increasingly in influence at the Kienthal Conference in April, 1916. From the Zimmerwald Left, which was maintained as a permanent international grouping, the path runs straight to the new Third or Communist International, finally constituted in 1919, into which the revolutionary left-wing of Zimmerwald was merged.

Thus, from 1914 onwards Lenin was the direct leader of international socialism, at first with only a nucleus

---

* V. I. Lenin, *The Imperialist War* (*Collected Works*, Vol. XVIII, International Publishers), pp. 61-64.
** *Ibid.*, pp. 76-83.

of supporters, but after a few years with millions following his leadership throughout the world.

Lenin's line on the War followed and applied the line of revolutionary Marxism to the concrete situation of the War of 1914-1918.   Through a host of articles, speeches, resolutions and brochures, (especially, *Socialism and War* in 1915; *The Collapse of the Second International* in 1915; the special study of the general character of the epoch, *Imperialism,* in 1916; and the series of articles, collected under the title *Against the Stream,* of 1914-16) , as well as through direct contact with the representatives of the movements of the leading countries, Lenin fought continuously for three main propositions:

First, that the War was not a war for "national defense," as the jingo ex-Socialist leaders falsely claimed, and on the strength of which claim the masses were drawn into the War, but an imperialist war: that is to say, a war of the great imperialist powers of finance-capitalist groups for world profits and world plunder, for territorial annexations, tribute and colonies (the subsequently revealed secret treaties of the Entente Powers, the Brest-Litovsk Treaty imposed by Germany, and the Versailles Treaty imposed by the victorious Entente fully confirmed the correctness of this analysis) . Marxism, Lenin insisted, was not necessarily opposed to any and every war, so long as social and national oppression remained: it recognized the necessity and justification of a revolutionary war (in defense of a socialist fatherland against capitalist attack) , or of a war of national liberation (as of the Indian or Chinese peoples against imperialism) .   But in the present imperialist war the working masses had no interest to kill one another for the profit of their masters: their interest was to unite against the imperialists.

Second, that the consequent line of the working class

in every country must be to fight their own imperialists, to transform the imperialist war into civil war, into war for the overthrow of the capitalist class and for the victory of socialism. There was no other way out from the cycle of world wars and universal destruction into which capitalism had now entered. The necessary consequence of this, that revolutionary agitation in war was equivalent to working for the defeat of "one's own" government, was clearly faced. To denounce only enemy imperialism and support "one's own" imperialism was nothing but support of imperialism. The test of a sincere and serious fight against imperialism was to fight "one's own" imperialist government. The workers, as Marx had said, and as all the ex-Socialist renegades now sought to deny, had no fatherland. The question of revolutionary national defense could only arise, when the workers had conquered possession of their own country.

Third, that the collapse of the Second International was no mere formal severance of relations between the Socialist parties owing to the War, to be healed by reunion after the War, nor an accidental betrayal by certain leaders, but the exposure and inevitable outcome of the opportunist degeneration of the old Socialist parties and their leadership. A new revolutionary working-class International would have to be built up, purged of opportunism. "The Second International is dead, long live the Third International!"

All these propositions were put forward by Lenin already in the first weeks of the War. With his invariable method of sharp and exact demarcation of the line of fight, leaving no possibility of confusion behind vaguely "internationalist" and "anti-war" phrases, Lenin marked out three tendencies in the international Socialist and labor movement as it developed under the conditions of war (most fully worked out in his "Tasks of the

Proletariat in Our Revolution" * in April, 1917, after the tendencies had completely revealed themselves):

First, the social-chauvinists—represented by the majority of the leaders of the official Social-Democratic parties in the various countries, Henderson, Scheidemann, Renaudel, etc. These are "Socialists in words and chauvinists in fact, people who are for 'national defense' in any imperialist war." Of these Lenin said shortly: "These men are our class enemies. They have gone over to the bourgeoisie."

Second, the social-pacifists or Center—represented by the Kautsky Social-Democratic minority in Germany, the Longuet minority in France, MacDonald, Snowden and the leaders of the Independent Labor Party in England, etc. "The 'center' does not call the workers to overthrow the capitalist government, but tries to persuade the present imperialist governments to conclude a democratic peace. . . . The 'center' insists on unity with the defencists on an international scale." Of these Lenin said: "The 'center' is a realm of sweet petit-bourgeois phrases, of internationalism in words, cowardly opportunism, and fawning before social-chauvinism in deeds."

Third, the revolutionary Internationalists—represented by the Spartacus group of Liebknecht and Rosa Luxemburg in Germany, and by the Bolsheviks, and by groups and individuals (e.g., John Maclean and Tom Mann in Britain) approaching towards their standpoint in other countries.

The core of Lenin's leadership on imperialist war was the slogan "transformation of the imperialist war into civil war." This slogan was derided and denounced on all sides, not merely by direct opponents, but also by

* V. I. Lenin, *The Revolution of 1917* (Collected Works, Vol. XX, International Publishers), Book I, pp. 130-157.

the majority even of the Socialist leaders who took part
in Zimmerwald, as the mad dream of an *émigré* out of
touch with realities.   But history was soon to show
where the realities lay, when the revolution broke out
in Russia in March, 1917.

4. THE VICTORY OF THE REVOLUTION IN RUSSIA

The Russian Revolution was from the outset a mass
revolt from below.   It was begun by the workers of
Petrograd striking and coming out on the streets under
the slogans, "Down with the War!" "Down with Tsarism!" and "Give us Bread!"   A continuously rising
movement of strikes and demonstrations reached its
height in the early days of March, when hundreds of
thousands of workers came on the streets.   The Cossacks
refused to strike down the workers.   The victory of
the Revolution was sealed when the soldiers sent to
shoot down the workers began in increasing numbers to
come over to the workers, and to assist in shooting down
the tsarist special police.   There was no alternative
before tsarism but abdication.

The long-delayed collapse of tsarism was only the
more complete because of the wholesale economic and
administrative disorganization and breakdown consequent on the War, the utter corruption and demoraliza-
tion of the upper classes, the unparalleled butchery on
the war fronts, the ruin of the peasantry and the starva-
tion of the masses in the towns.

The February Revolution * was the achievement of
the working masses and of the soldiers alone and of no

* The revolution which overthrew the Tsar took place in February,
old calendar, March, new calendar, and is known as the February
Revolution.   The Bolshevik Revolution which overthrew the Pro-
visional Government and established the Soviet Power, took place in
October, old calendar, November, new calendar, and is known as the
October Revolution.—*Ed.*

other. All power was in fact in the hands of the workers and soldiers in the days of March, if they had known how to use it and been clear of their aims. The aims of the mass revolution in March were in essence, in the germ, the same as those that finally reached realization in the October Revolution: the aims of peace, of bread, of land, and of a new social order. But there was not yet any clear political consciousness, any consciousness of the necessary path to the realization of these aims, save among the still small Bolshevik vanguard. Therefore a process of intense political development had to take place, during the eight months from March to November, before these aims could be realized.

The eight months from the first to the second Russian Revolution of 1917 were thus eight months of rapid unfolding of the class struggle, of successively clearer revelation of the rôle of each class and its repretatives, and of the intensive political development and awakening of the masses up to the final point of the conscious conquest of power by the workers in union with the peasants and establishment of their own form of government. The decisive rôle within this process of development of the masses was the leadership of the political vanguard of the working class, the Bolshevik Party, which grew in strength with the advance of the masses, from a minority to a majority position, and carried the advance forward, and which organized and led the conquest of power and formed the new government. The decisive rôle within this leadership of the Bolshevik Party was the leadership of Lenin.

The Petrograd Soviet of Workers' and Soldiers' Deputies was formed immediately on the victory of the February Revolution. Similar Soviets sprang up rapidly all over the country, and were the natural democratic instrument of the masses, far more democratic than any parliament. But the Soviets had at first no conscious intention of taking over the functions of government.

The politically inexperienced masses in the Soviets or Councils of Workers' and Soldiers' Deputies put their faith at first in the Menshevik and Socialist-Revolutionary politicians; the Bolsheviks were at the beginning a minority, based only on the class-conscious workers. The Menshevik and Socialist-Revolutionary leaders in their turn hung at the tail of the bourgeoisie, and begged the most prominent bourgeois politicians to form a government. Thus the bourgeoisie, who had played no part in the Revolution, were able to form a Provisional "Revolutionary" Government under Prince Lvov and Milyukov, the Cadet (Constitutional-Democrat) leader, with one representative of the so-called "Labor" group, Kerensky, connected with the extreme right Socialist-Revolutionaries, as a "popular" representative. In this way a régime of a "dual power" was established. On the one side, the Provisional Government of bourgeois ministers carried on the old tsarist machine and imperialist war aims, but with diminishing obedience from the workers and soldiers. On the other side, the Soviets, which had far more real power, voted decisions which aroused the horror of the Provisional Government and of the General Staff, but which were obeyed, such as the famous Order No. 1, establishing control by elected soldiers' committees in the army. Meanwhile the right-wing leaders of the Soviets continued to dance attendance on the Provisional Government, begged them to adopt "democratic" war aims, etc.

It was obvious that this dual power could not continue long. One class or the other must rule. The eight months constituted, in fact, a succession of shocks and attacks from either side, in the course of which it became increasingly clear that there were only two alternatives: either complete conquest of power by the workers and peasants, the establishment of the Soviet power, as advocated by the Bolsheviks, or complete counter-revolution, as plotted by General Kornilov and Kerensky. The petty-bourgeois representatives, the Menshevik and Socialist-Revolutionary leaders, who vacillated between the two, inevitably lost more and more their foothold.

Lenin arrived in Petrograd from Switzerland on April 16. The Entente Powers, who facilitated the passage to Russia of a host of tame "Socialist" leaders in their service, such as Henderson, Thorne, Albert Thomas, etc., and the return of all right-wing Menshevik and Socialist-Revolutionary *émigrés,* did all in their power to block the passage of the revolutionary Socialists in exile, and, in particular, of the Bolshevik leaders. Lenin and his fellow *émigrés* were compelled to take advantage of the contradictions of imperialism and, after elaborate negotiations, and with a signed document of approval from prominent international Socialist leaders, to pass through Germany in a sealed train. This incident was made abundant use of by his political enemies after his return, including the Kerensky Government, to prove that Lenin and the Bolsheviks were "German agents." The fact is only worth noticing as a measure of the intellectual level of bourgeois propaganda against the Bolsheviks. It may be noted that Ludendorff in his Memoirs subsequently recorded that he had in fact hoped that the passage of the Bolsheviks would assist the disruption of the Russian military power, but that he only too late realized his error, that its final consequence was the disruption of the German Empire. The meaning of revolutionary internationalism, fighting for a new world order, remains a closed book to the bourgeoisie.

Lenin had from the first, already before he left

Switzerland, a completely clear view of the relation of class forces in the Revolution, and of the necessary path forward.   In a letter of March 16, on the receipt of the first scanty telegrams of news of the Revolution, he wrote that the task now was "the conquest of power by the Soviets of Workers' Deputies."   On March 17th, in his first draft theses, he wrote:

Only a workers' government, basing itself, first, on the vast majority of the peasant population, the rural workers and the poorest peasants; second, on an alliance with the revolutionary workers of the warring countries, can give peace, bread and complete freedom to the people.

On April 8, in his *Letters from Afar,* he defined the task

(1) To find the surest road leading to the next stage of the revolution or to the second revolution, which revolution (2) shall transfer the state power from the government of landowners and capitalists (the Guchkovs, Lvovs, Milyukovs, Kerenskys) to a government of the workers and poorest peasants. (3) The latter government must be organized on the model of the Soviet of Workers' and Peasants' Deputies. . . .

Only such a government, he wrote, could carry through the fight for peace, the confiscation of the land from the landowners, the control of industry, all which steps

would represent the *transition to Socialism,* which in Russia cannot be realized immediately, directly, without transition measures, which, however, is perfectly realizable and urgently needed as a result of such transition measures.

At the time of his arrival in Russia, five weeks after the victory of the first revolution, Lenin was faced with the position that the Soviets were overwhelmingly dominated by the petty-bourgeois Menshevik and Socialist-Revolutionary leaders, who in their turn hung at the tail of the bourgeois government.

In the face of this situation Lenin, immediately on

his arrival, issued and began the fight for his famous April Theses on "The Tasks of the Proletariat in the Present Revolution," which marked the path ahead to the October Revolution.* These theses covered ten points, which may be summarized briefly as follows:

1. No concession to "revolutionary defencism" under a capitalist government; a "revolutionary war" can be agreed to only *after* the workers and poorest peasantry are in power, all annexations are renounced, and a complete break made with the interests of capital.

2. Recognition of the present stage of the revolution as a transition to the second stage, the conquest of power by the proletariat and poorest peasantry.

3. No support to the Provisional Government.

4. Task of the Bolsheviks, while a minority in the Soviets, to conduct "patient, systematic and persistent" propaganda to win the majority from the policy of the petty-bourgeois opportunist leaders to the policy of the transference of state power to the Soviets.

5. Not a parliamentary republic, but a republic of Soviets of Workers' and Peasants' Deputies.

6. Nationalization of the land and management by peasants' Soviets; separate organization of poorest peasants and agricultural laborers.

7. Nationalization of the banks into one central bank under the Workers' Soviet control.

8. "Not the 'introduction' of socialism as an immediate task, but the immediate placing of the Soviet of Workers' Delegates in control of social production and distribution of goods."

9. Party Congress, and revision of program.

10. Creation of a new, revolutionary International.

It is only necessary to examine this April program, more especially in its full text, to see its extreme closeness to the subsequent realization in the October Revolution and the further tasks of the Soviet régime. All the slanders and calumnies, as well as honest miscon-

---

* All the letters referred to as well as the Theses are included in *The Revolution of 1917*, which contains all of Lenin's writings and speeches between March and July, 1917.

ceptions, which it has been attempted to build up around the October Revolution—the supposed conception of the conquest of power by a minority; the supposed rejection of the Constituent Assembly and parliamentary democratic forms only after the event, for reasons of expediency or for anti-democratic reasons; the supposed idea of immediately introducing socialism —all are refuted beforehand by the April program, and can only be repeated by those who are either ignorant of the facts or who deliberately conceal them.

The April Theses burst like dynamite through the fog of confusion which was growing up after the February Revolution, and which was threatening to engulf the Russian Revolution in the same fate as later overtook the German, if the path of the opportunist Socialists had been followed. The real issues of the Revolution were laid bare. Lenin's program was universally denounced by political opponents of every shade as anarchist ravings; it was derided by Plekhanov, the old founder of social-democracy in Russia, now turned into a vulgar patriot, as "delirium."

Nevertheless, its inevitable necessity and reflection of the real needs of the masses was rapidly to win for it ever wider numbers of supporters. Within three weeks Lenin's program was unanimously adopted by the Congress of the Bolshevik Party on May 5-12. Within the next few months this program was to become, in fact, the program of the overwhelming majority of the workers and soldiers throughout the country.

The successive conflicts and sharpening of the issues, consequent on the dual power, forced the development forward. In May the attempt of Milyukov, as Foreign Minister, to proclaim continuity of the old imperialist war aims led to such overwhelming mass demonstrations that Milyukov and Guchkov had to go, and a new Coalition Ministry was established with Kerensky as

War Minister and with the direct participation of the
right-wing Socialist leaders. But this in turn meant the
further exposure of the right Socialist leaders and their
alienation from the masses, since they could only pursue
the same policy of subjection to the bourgeoisie, and,
above all, to Anglo-French capital. Under this pressure
they were compelled to order the useless and sanguinary
July offensive, in contradiction to all their peace
speeches. The July offensive in turn roused the anger
of the masses to fever heat, and resulted in the armed
demonstration of July in Petrograd, which showed that
the workers, soldiers and sailors of the Petrograd region
were ready to advance to the conquest of power; only
the Bolshevik leadership, which knew that the position was not yet ripe and that Petrograd would have
run the danger of being isolated, was able to hold
them in.

After the days of July the entire governmental forces,
police, press and propaganda were turned against the
Bolsheviks; many of the leaders were imprisoned; Lenin
was charged by the Kerensky government with high
treason as a "German agent," forged documents of the
usual fantastic nature being published in abundance to
prove it; he was compelled to go underground and
continue his leadership from conditions of illegality
thenceforth until the victory of the revolution, or he
would have met the fate of Liebknecht; many attempts
were planned by the officer-cliques to kill him. The
"Socialist" ministers were thus playing straight into the
hands of counter-revolution; and in September inevitably followed the attempted coup of General
Kornilov (appointed Commander-in-Chief by Kerensky), who marched with his Savage Division on Petrograd to suppress the revolution.

In the face of the Kornilov attack, the whole strength
of the Soviets awoke to action: the Bolsheviks, and the

armed workers, sailors and soldiers who followed the
Bolsheviks, threw themselves in the front of the defense.
The Kornilov *putsch* collapsed ignominiously. But the
effect was enormously to raise the authority of the
Bolsheviks as the true leaders and defenders of the revolution, and to discredit the Provisional Government
and Kerensky, who was found to have been in very
close secret relations with Kornilov up to the last moment. It now became more than ever clear that either
the revolution must be completed by the establishment
of the Soviet power, or must surrender to extreme
counter-revolution: there was no middle course.

Through this succession of events and developments
the Bolsheviks won more and more completely the overwhelming majority of the masses behind them, in Petrograd, Moscow, and the big centers, in the trade unions,
in the northern armies, in the Baltic fleet. The Bolsheviks won the majority in the Petrograd and Moscow
Soviets by the beginning of September. At the "Democratic Conference" summoned by Kerensky in September, the trade union delegation, the Soviet delegation,
and the national groups all voted overwhelmingly for
the Bolshevik line of opposition to the Coalition Government. The Moscow municipal elections, which in
July had shown 70 per cent of the votes for the Mensheviks and Socialist-Revolutionaries, in September
gave these only 18 per cent, and 51 per cent to the
Bolsheviks. Finally, the Second All-Russian Soviet
Congress, elected from all over Russia under the auspices of the old right-wing Central Executive Committee in October, and meeting under their auspices on
November 7, showed: 390 Bolsheviks, 179 Left Socialist-
Revolutionaries (joining with the Bolsheviks), 35 Internationalist Mensheviks, and only 51 Mensheviks and
Right Socialist-Revolutionaries. There was no question that by October, and even by September, the masses

had declared overwhelmingly and, above all, in all the big centers, for the Bolsheviks. This was the basis of the Bolshevik Revolution, and of the completeness of its victory, on November 7.

Already by September Lenin was urging that the moment had come for the final stage of armed insurrection. During October his warnings became ever more urgent, lest the favorable moment of the height of the wave should pass and give way to mass disillusionment and the consequent triumph of the counter-revolution.

The responsible leaders of our party are confronted with a gigantic task; if they do not carry it out, it will mean a total collapse of the internationalist proletarian movement. The situation is such that delay truly means death. (Letter of October 21, 1917, to the Bolsheviks in the Northern Soviet Regional Congress.*)

Again and again through the manifold urgent letters and messages of this period sounds the note: "Delay means death."

With all my power I wish to persuade the comrades that now everything hangs on a hair, that on the order of the day are questions that are not solved by conferences, by congresses (even by Congresses of Soviets), but only by the people, by the masses, by the struggle of armed masses. (Letter of November 6, 1917, to the Central Committee.**)

On October 23, the Central Committee of the Bolshevik Party took the final decision for the insurrection by a vote of all against two. On the night of November 6 and the morning of November 7, the conquest of power took place with complete orderliness; the Provisional Government had no longer any support in any quarter to be able to make resistance; the Bolshevik Revolution was, in contrast with the February Revo-

* V. I. Lenin, *Toward the Seizure of Power*, Book II, pp. 100-105.
** *Ibid.*, pp. 144-145.

lution, almost completely bloodless, the most bloodless revolution in history. The Second All-Russian Congress of Soviets took over the power as the sovereign body, and appointed the Council of People's Commissars, consisting of Bolsheviks, under the leadership of Lenin, as the mandatories of the new power of the working masses. The dictatorship of the proletariat, in alliance with the mass of the peasantry, was realized.

It is essential to understand the overwhelming majority support of the population for the Bolshevik Revolution in order to understand why the final transformation was able to take place with such speed, apparent ease and complete lack of resistance. The final transformation was only the culmination of a long process. The Bolshevik Revolution was, in fact, the most democratic revolution in history. The myth of its "anti-democratic" character is based on the dissolution of the Constituent Assembly in January, 1918: but the April program had long before made clear that the Constituent Assembly could not be more than a means of agitation within the bourgeois régime, and that as a democratic instrument it was far below the level of the Soviets. In addition the lists on which the election took place, which treated the Socialist-Revolutionary Party as a single party under right leadership, when in fact the overwhelming majority had broken with this leadership and entered into alliance with the Bolsheviks in a coalition, were out of date and no longer representative. The Second Soviet Congress elections provided the clearest demonstration of the majority basis of the Bolsheviks before the seizure of power. The subsequent civil war, when the counter-revolutionary generals could only organize resistance with foreign arms, subsidies and troops, and the complete defeat of these, in the face of all the odds, and in the face of the combined efforts of the strongest military powers in the world, afforded the final demonstration in practice of the mass basis of the Bolshevik Revolution.

The eight months from March to November reveal the highest level and most intense tempo of Lenin's revolutionary leadership. His writings during this period constitute the permanent classic for Marxists of leadership in the midst of a revolution and of the art of insurrection. At the same time, in the midst of the conflict, he completed one of his most important theoretical works, *State and Revolution*, clearing the line of revolutionary Marxism on the urgent questions of the form and content of the state and the meaning of the social revolution, and destroying the opportunist distortions which had grown up in the Social-Democratic movement.

The tasks which were now to confront him in the succeeding years were even bigger tasks—but to be cut short by death.

5. THE LEADERSHIP OF THE WORLD REVOLUTION

In the beginning of the twentieth century Lenin had written:

History has now confronted us with an immediate task which is *more revolutionary than all the immediate tasks* that confront the proletariat of any other country. The fulfillment of this task, the destruction of the most powerful bulwark, not only of European, but also (it may be said) of Asiatic reaction, places the Russian proletariat in the vanguard of the international revolutionary proletariat.*

The realization of this prediction a decade and a half after these words were written took place in a far more complicated and difficult world situation than any prediction could have foreseen. The Russian prole-

* *What Is to Be Done?* p. 30.

tariat did, in fact, become by the Revolution of 1917, and decisively by the October Revolution, the vanguard of the international proletariat. But it had to assume leadership in the midst of the condition of the World War; it had to assume leadership with its own base in Russia ruined and disorganized to complete breakdown by tsarism and the war; and it had to assume leadership in advance and in danger of isolation, while the other battalions were not yet ready and the revolution hung fire in western and central Europe.

Nevertheless, this gigantic task and world historic responsibility was faced without flinching, realistically, and in its fullest magnitude. The comprehension of the character of this task, and the discovery of the methods of its fulfillment in the completely new unforeseeable conditions, sprang above all from Lenin. To lead the world revolution, to fight the ring of imperialist enemies, and to build the new order in Russia —these were the simultaneous aspects of the hundred-fold task which now fell upon the Russian proletariat under the leadership of the Bolshevik Party and of Lenin. To every aspect of this task Lenin now set all the powers of his mind and will, as leader of the Soviet Government, as leader of the Communist Party, and as leader of the Communist International, during the momentous years 1917-1923, until the burden broke and smashed him, body and brain, and consigned him to early death, with his work unfinished, but with the main lines laid down for his successors to complete.

The work of Lenin during this period outstrips any summary biography. It ranges in its volume over the whole field of world politics, of the civil war, of relations with the imperialist powers, of building the new Soviet democracy, of building the new economic order towards socialism, of relations with the peasantry, of the Communist Party, of the new Communist Inter-

national, of direct participation and leadership in the
working-class movement of every country in the world.
Alongside the host of speeches, reports and pamphlets
of this period, his two books written during these critical years are, characteristically enough, devoted to the
guidance of the international working-class movement,
The Proletarian Revolution and the Renegade Kautsky
and *"Left-Wing" Communism, an Infantile Disorder:
an Attempt at a Popular Discussion on Marxist Strategy
and Tactics.*

The victory of the Bolshevik Revolution in Russia
was the opening, the first stage, of the world socialist
revolution.

But the development of the world revolution was
destined to prove far lengthier and more complicated
than Lenin and the Bolsheviks had hoped when they
opened the battle in November, 1917. At the outset
they had hoped for the rapid spread of the revolution
to the leading European countries in the next few
months. The peace appeal to all the warring governments and peoples which was one of the first acts of
the new Soviet power in the first hours of its existence,
no less than the public conduct of the Brest-Litovsk
peace negotiations with German imperialism during
December and January were all directed to awakening
the masses to end the imperialist slaughter. A powerful
strike movement developed in Germany and Austria
during January, 1918. But despite the growing unrest
of the war-weary masses in Germany, France and
Britain, reflected in the rising strike movement and
military revolts, the more strongly organized ruling
machine of the bourgeoisie in these countries, with the
aid of the jingo social-democracy, was able to maintain
control. Therefore the Brest-Litovsk Peace, the "rob-
ber's peace," had to be signed in March, 1918. It was
only after a long and sharp division in the party that

the necessity to sign this peace was finally recognized as the sole means to maintain the Soviet power. The Left Socialist-Revolutionaries, who had entered into a coalition in the Soviet Government after the conquest of power, withdrew in the summer of 1918 on this issue, and endeavored to raise a fight against the Soviet Government, but only revealed their own lack of mass support. Advocating the signing of the Brest-Litovsk Treaty before the Soviet Central Executive Committee in March, 1918, Lenin said:

At present we are in a desperately difficult situation; our ally cannot rush to our aid. The international proletariat cannot come just now, but it will come.

Lenin's confidence was justified. In November, 1918, the German proletariat rose, overthrew Kaiserism, annulled the Brest-Litovsk Treaty and ended the World War. The world revolutionary wave of 1918-21 began.

The ending of the imperialist war only gave place to the series of civil wars and interventionist wars with which western imperialism sought to destroy the Soviet Republic, and which had already begun on every side during the last year of the imperialist war. German invasions and depredations during 1918; British, French, American and Japanese invasions on every front during 1918 to 1920; the supporting, arming and subsidizing of counter-revolutionary generals and brigands; and sabotage, conspiracy and assassination (on August 30, 1918, Lenin was shot and heavily wounded; although he fought his way to recovery and resumption of work, the consequences of this wounding were in great part responsible for his early death) : these were the weapons of world imperialism against the young Soviet Republic.

The German Revolution ended the depredations of German imperialism; but the Entente attacks became

only the more intensified in 1919. The Allied Powers
at Versailles recognized the dictator Kolchak as Regent
of Russia. The British in North Russia; the British
and French at Odessa in the South; Yudenich at the
gates of Petrograd; Kolchak in Siberia; Petlura in the
Ukraine; Denikin in the South: all were armed and
directed by western imperialism to overthrow Bolshevism.

Nevertheless, all the millionfold efforts of imperialism to overthrow the Soviet régime collapsed. They
collapsed, first, because of the mass resistance of the
population in Russia, not only of the Red Army and
industrial workers, but of the peasantry in the regions
the Whites overran, and for whom the White restoration meant the loss of the land; second, because of the
refusal of the British and French troops to carry on
the shameful war (revolt of the French Black Sea Fleet,
unrest in the British troops in North Russia, impossibility of sending more troops); and third, because of
the active struggle of the British and French workers
against the war of intervention. The world revolutionary wave was reaching its height in 1919. In the spring
of 1919 the Communist International was founded. The
international working class defeated the war of imperialism on the Soviet Republic.

By the end of 1920, with the defeat of Wrangel, the
main counter-revolutionary and interventionist forces
were all defeated. The climax and turning point of
the direct war of revolution and counter-revolution was
reached in the summer of 1920 with the Polish War.
Poland, with military supplies and guidance from
Britain and France, had launched an offensive against
the Soviet Republic in the spring of 1920, despite the
repeated Soviet offers of an armistice and negotiations.
The Polish offensive was overwhelmingly defeated, and
gave place to a revolutionary offensive which reached

to within a few miles of Warsaw. The offensive to Warsaw was from a military strategic point of view open to criticism and had to be followed by a retreat; but Lenin took the direct responsibility in advocating this offensive, which nearly turned the fortunes of the European revolution, for political reasons. Just as the Brest-Litovsk Treaty and subsequent new economic policy showed the ability of Lenin's leadership to retreat (for which reason these two have been taken by all bourgeois and reformist writers as the height of his statesmanship, as if they were more important than the Bolshevik Revolution), so the advance on Warsaw showed his equal readiness to take the most daring offensive when the situation offered even a chance against odds to gain by it. Despite its subsequent defeat, Lenin judged the offensive a gain (Report to the All-Russian Communist Party Conference, September, 1920), first, because it demonstrated the strength of the Soviet régime to western imperialism and put a check on the policy of constant ·attacks, and second, because of the enormous stimulus it gave to the European working-class movement, as shown in the British Council of Action.

A completely new world situation developed from the beginning of 1921. On the one hand the international working class had been able to defeat the attack of imperialism on the Soviet Republic. On the other hand, the international working class had not been able to overthrow imperialism outside the Soviet Republic. In consequence, a temporary "equilibrium" or "balance of forces" resulted, which might last for a shorter or longer period, during which it was necessary to prepare and organize the working-class forces so long as the "respite" lasted, until a new attack of imperialism developed or a new world revolutionary wave. How was this new situation to be met? It was to the problems of this new period, opening in 1921, and still continuing, though now visibly approaching its close, that Lenin gave his final leadership to the world working class.

In the first place, a completely new turn was necessary in the Soviet Republic. With the ending of the civil wars, the original plans of economic construction, through workers' state control of production to the organization of socialism, already set out with complete clearness both before and immediately after the Bolshevik Revolution, had now to be resumed. The blockade and the civil wars had interrupted all these plans and compelled the system of "War Communism," *i.e.*, universal requisitioning and rationing, but no organization of socialist production. It was now necessary to end this system; such incidents as the Kronstadt revolt and the Tambov revolt in the beginning of 1921 showed the urgency. Accordingly, in March, 1921, the New Economic Policy was introduced. This replaced the requisitioning by the agricultural tax, and restored a limited freedom of small-scale private trading, while the workers' state retained the "economic heights," the monopoly of foreign trade, banking, transport, and large-scale industry. In this way the controlled advance to an increasing proportion of socialist organization of production could be systematically carried forward.

At the time, and for some years thereafter, all ignorant capitalist and reformist comment universally hailed the New Economic Policy or "Nep" as the return to capitalism and abandonment of socialism. It was, of course, nothing of the kind, as Lenin made fully clear at the time, but on the contrary the method of the conscious and systematic advance to socialism. To-day this is clear to all, and the old prophecies of the victory of private capitalism through Nep have already passed into the dustbin of history, now that the process of systematic development has reached the stage of large-scale socialist construction through the Five-Year Plan. In the time of Lenin it was still possible for the capitalist propagandists to point to the ruin and destruction caused by tsarism and the civil wars (notably the famine of 1921, which took place in the regions that had been devastated by the White brigands) as evidence of the "bankruptcy of socialism" in contrast to capitalist "prosperity" in America and western Europe. To-day when four years of the world economic crisis of capitalism have demonstrated universal declining production, unemployment and chaos in every country of the capitalist world, while the Soviet Union alone has doubled and trebled its production at a rate unequalled in history, this propaganda is no longer possible. Yet all this development was already implicit in the lines of policy laid down by Lenin, although he could not live to see it.

At the same time, it was necessary for the international working-class movement in the new period from 1921 to make a turn and "organize the retreat" preparatory to new advance. The newly-formed Communist Parties were required to pass from the previous directly revolutionary situation to the task of building up and organizing their strength in the daily struggle and winning the majority of the working class. To this task the Third Congress of the Communist International was devoted in the summer of 1921, under the close leadership of Lenin. In December of the same year the policy of the united working-class front was developed under Lenin's guidance.

How long would this new situation of the "balance" or "breathing-space," with the necessary tasks of organization and preparation of the working-class forces, last? It was impossible to foretell. At the end of 1921 Lenin declared:

A balance has been attained, a highly unstable one, but certainly a balance. Will it last long? I don't know; nor do I think that any one can tell. We must, therefore, show the greatest possible wariness. (Speech to the Ninth All-Russian Soviet Congress, December 23, 1921.)

And again in November, 1922, at the Fourth Congress of the Communist International, in one of the last speeches that he was able to make to the world, Lenin said:

Now for the first time we have the possibility of learning. I do not know how long this possibility will last. I do not know how long the capitalist powers will give us the opportunity of learning in peace and quietude. But we must utilize every moment in which we are free from war, that we may learn, and learn from the bottom up. . . .

I am confident that in this sense we have to say, not only for the Russians, but for the foreigners as well, that the most important thing for us all in the period now opening is to learn. We Russians have to learn in the general sense. You have to learn in the special sense that you may gain a genuine understanding of the organization, structure, method and substance of revolutionary work. If you do this, I am confident that the prospects for the world revolution are not merely favorable, but splendid.

These were among the last words of Lenin. Already in the spring of 1922 the fatal illness that was to end his life had shown itself in the paralysis of his right arm and leg. He fought it through; he resumed work; but he had to complain that he could no longer win the same response from his overdriven physique and brain. In the spring of 1923 came a second and heavier attack. In May, 1923, he wrote his last article, "On Co-operation," pointing the way forward to the "establishment of a fully socialized society" for which "we have all the means requisite. . . . Of course we have not yet established a socialist society, but we have all the means requisite for its establishment." The unequal battle for life and consciousness dragged on over months. On January 21, 1924, he died.

The work of Lenin's last period, the period of the leadership of the world revolution, from 1917 to 1923, is like a gigantic torso. In the previous periods he put forward each time at the outset a precise formulation of the task to be accomplished, which appeared to his contemporaries at the beginning like a madman's dream, and accomplished it with exact completeness. He formulated the conception of the Bolshevik Party, of a workers' revolutionary party, rising to the full heights of political revolutionary leadership, yet never turning into a sect, but linked to the masses and their everyday struggle and life by a million ties. This conception was realized in the Bolshevik Party, when in every other country social-democracy turned either into the slough of opportunism or into sectarian dogmatism. At the beginning of the War he formulated his conception of the transformation of the imperialist war into civil war for the overthrow of imperialism. This transformation was realized with exact completeness in 1917. At the beginning of the Russian Revolution he formulated his conception of the advance to the second revolution, to the establishment of the Soviet Power, of the dictatorship of the proletariat in alliance with the peasantry. This second revolution was realized with exact completeness in the October Revolution. At the beginning of the last period he formulated the task of the simultaneous advance to the world revolution and the building of socialism in the Soviet Union. This task he could only begin, laying down the lines and methods of advance. At the moment when his leadership was reaching its greatest height throughout the whole world, to transform the whole world, death cut short his work. It remains for others to complete his work.

CHAPTER III

THE TEACHINGS OF LENIN

ALIKE in direct theoretical exposition, and in his practical life, Lenin gave a clear answer to the problems confronting humanity in our epoch. He did not invent this answer as a new discovery out of his inner consciousness; he was no fabricator of a new system, sect or religion. He built on the entire previous work of human thought and culture at its highest point in Marxism. But he brought Marxism to new life in relation to the living problems and tasks of the present epoch. He found Marxism endangered and even enfeebled by a suffocating overweight of pedants, cowards and small philistine minds such as were incapable of carrying forward its mighty work. He left Marxism a stronger revolutionary power than ever before, the recognized strongest power of our epoch, and already realizing itself in triumphant revolutionary practice.

The teachings of Lenin, like those of Marxism, of which Leninism is the continuation in our period, cannot be confined in any closed system of formulæ. Not only is their richness, many-sidedness and life lost in any such summary: but such formal treatment is directly contrary to their dialectical character. The dialectical approach analyzes every living concrete situation in its own distinctive character and relationships, and draws out the understanding of the general social laws of development in the particular concrete manifestation and the consequent specific tasks of action. That is why the understanding of Marxism and Leninism can only be reached, not through any textbooks, but only, first, by the close study of Marx's and Lenin's lives, writings and activities in relation to the concrete historical situations which they handled, and secondly, by direct participation in the revolutionary movement, consciously breaking with the old forms of thought, and fighting to carry forward their principles to the living present situation. Lenin and Marx left no hand-books of Leninism or Marxism; they revealed their principle only in the course of direct handling of defi-nite urgent problems in concrete fields of human prac-tice and theory.

In consequence, any short notes that may be here given on a few of the main conceptions of Lenin's teaching cannot be treated as in any way a summary or substitute for the real teachings of Lenin.

1. THE GENERAL WORLD OUTLOOK OF LENIN

With Lenin, as with Marx, the immediate revolu-tionary outlook and practice in relation to the particu-lar period in which each lived was based on a fully thought-out wider general world outlook and under-standing.

Lenin constantly insisted that communism cannot be regarded as a special body of doctrines or dogmas, of "ready-made conclusions" to be learnt from text-books, but can only be understood as the outcome of the whole of human science and culture, on the basis of an exact study of all that previous ages, including espe-cially capitalist society, had achieved. Speaking to the Third Congress of the Communist Youth in Russia in 1920, he said:

It would be a very serious mistake to suppose that one can become a Communist without making one's own the treasures of human knowledge. It would be mistaken to imagine that it is enough to adopt the Communist formulæ and conclusions of Communist science without mastering that sum-total of different branches of knowledge, the final outcome of which is communism. . . .

Communism becomes an empty phrase, a mere façade, and the Communist a mere bluffer, if he has not worked over in his consciousness the whole inheritance of human knowledge.

Therefore he urged the youth

to acquire the whole sum of human knowledge, and to acquire it in such a way that communism will not be something learnt by heart, but something which you have thought out yourselves, something which forms the inevitable conclusion from the point of view of modern education.

In the same way he wrote with reference to the controversy on "proletarian culture":

Marxism won its world-historic significance as the ideology of the revolutionary proletariat, because it did not reject out and out the most valuable achievements of the bourgeois epoch, but on the contrary made its own and worked over anew all that was of value in the more than two thousand years of development of human thought. ("Draft Resolution on Proletarian Culture," 1920.)

Lenin thus saw in Marxism, not some special "system" of dogmas, but the culmination of the many streams of previous human thought, development and advance to a scientific outlook. Marxism brought for the first time the completely scientific, simultaneously theoretical and practical, approach, not merely to one or two isolated departments of knowledge, but to the whole of life and existence.

The outlook of Marxism is the outlook of dialectical materialism, of which something has been said in the first chapter on the Epoch of Lenin. Lenin was a dialectical materialist. His thought and action in every problem and in every relation of life, in the aims he set himself, and in the methods of their achievement, were completely governed by this basic understanding of existence and life, of the rôle of human beings, of the laws of historical development, of the necessary forms and methods of advance within the conditions of class society, and of the future world order to be achieved of associated humanity in control of its destiny. This gave him his strength against the shortsighted, interest-ridden and illusion-soaked statesmen and theorists of the bourgeois order. The achievement of his life was a powerful demonstration of the correctness and efficacy of dialectical materialism.

But dialectical materialism is no closed metaphysical "system"—to become out-of-date, as all systems inevitably must. Dialectical materialism, as Engels pointed out, requires to be constantly renewed in every age, with every advance of science and of concrete knowledge. This task, also, Lenin carried out, especially in his *Materialism and Empirio-Criticism*. Here he carried forward the understanding of dialectical materialism in relation to the new problems of science of the twentieth century, and fought the reactionary idealist mystical-religious tendencies which were increasingly creeping in under the protection of many bourgeois scientists.

On the one hand, Lenin brought to new clearness the understanding of materialism as the necessary basis of the scientific outlook. He fought without mercy religion and all the allies of religion: all the subjective religious and semi-religious "idealist" outlooks and illusions which enslave the mind and are, in fact, as he insisted, even in their most "modern" and pseudo-scientific trappings, nothing but forms of "clericalism" —that is, of apologetics of the existing order as divinely and mysteriously ordained, maintenance of servitude, and preventing of clear thinking and facing of reality.

At the same time Lenin showed how the old passive mechanical materialism, which had been the basis of the early scientists, was inadequate to comprehend reality in all its complex character, and therefore inevitably, with the advance of scientific knowledge, left the scientists in confusion and at the mercy of idealism. Only the materialist dialectic could show the way forward.

We must understand that no natural science, no materialism whatever, can hold out in the struggle against bourgeois ideas and the restoration of bourgeois philosophy without a solid philosophical basis. In order to give aid to this struggle and help to carry it out to its successful conclusion, the natural scientist must be a *modern* materialist—a conscious adherent of that materialism which Marx represents; that is, he must be a *dialectical* materialist. . . .
Modern natural scientists will find (if they will seek and if we can learn to help them) in the materialist interpretation of Hegelian dialectics a number of answers to those philosophical questions which the revolution in natural science has brought to the front, and which cause the intellectual admirers of bourgeois fashions to "slip" into the reactionary camp. ("The Meaning of Militant Materialism," 1922.)

"The decisive thing in Marxism," declared Lenin, "is its revolutionary dialectic" ("Concerning our Revolution"). Dialectical materialism destroys the old barriers between theory and practice. Its essential character as a world outlook is not only to discover the nature of reality, but to transform reality. Hence its revolutionary character. This unity of theory and practice, this completely dialectical approach to all problems, is most powerfully shown in the whole life of Lenin. There has been no such example in history of a completely conscious, controlled and theoretically illumined activity, directed to great objective aims, not drawn from arbitrary subjective notions, but from a scientific understanding of the world process and of human needs.

In this way, in the whole character and realization of his life, Lenin points the way forward to the new type of humanity of the future.

2. THE THEORY OF OUR EPOCH—IMPERIALISM

The basis of Marxist or Communist activity in a given stage is necessarily a clear analysis of the character of that stage, its forces and conflicts, and the consequent line of advance.

In the widest sense, Marx had laid bare the character of the capitalist stage of human society, had analyzed its laws of motion, had shown its advance to increasing concentration of capital, division of classes, mass impoverishment and growing crises, and had shown its necessary outcome in the proletarian revolution and the dictatorship of the proletariat to organize the classless socialist society.

But in the lifetime of Marx this formulation of the proletarian revolution and the dictatorship of the proletariat necessarily remained—with the sole exception of the advance indication of the Paris Commune—a theoretical formulation for the future. The practical task to which he had to give his leadership was the task of the preparation and organization of the working-class forces under the conditions of still ascendant capitalism.

Only after the death of Marx, in the period of Lenin, capitalism enters into its final dying stage, and the proletarian revolution begins.

At first the new stage into which capitalism was entering after the death of Marx was not clearly understood even by many Marxists. A host of new phenomena in all directions began to appear, and their underlying principles were not clear; many supposed Marxists began to claim that the new facts had disproved the expectations of Marx, and that revision was necessary. The growth of joint-stock capitalism replacing the old personally-owned businesses they saw as the "democratization of capital." They pointed to the spread of social reform legislation and to improved standards in western Europe and America as disproof of Marx's contentions of increasing class antagonism and mass misery. At the same time they were disturbed at other new developments of policy which were happening at the same time, seemingly in contradiction to this spread of "social liberalism," at the enormous growth of armaments and militarism, at rising tariff policies, at rapidly increasing colonial plunder raids and violence in all parts of the world; these tendencies they deprecated as contrary to the spirit of the age, and due to a mistaken understanding by the capitalists of their own interests. Such was the opportunist "liberal-socialist" outlook up to 1914, with which orthodox Marxism was in conflict.

It was Lenin who first brought out to complete clearness the character of the new epoch as a whole, and laid bare its laws of motion, with final completeness in his *Imperialism* (1916).*

He analyzed all the symptoms of the new epoch down to their basis in monopoly capitalism. The free trade capitalism which Marx had analyzed of competitive, relatively small-scale businesses, had developed, as Marx had foretold it must, by the constant victory of large-scale over small-scale and increasing concentration of capital, to monopoly capitalism as the dominant modern form, or finance-capital: that is to say, large syndicates and trusts, fusing bank capital and industrial capital under a single direction, and working in close coöperation with the state machine.

To this new stage of monopoly capitalism corre-

* V. I. Lenin, *Imperialism—the Highest Stage of Capitalism* (International Publishers).

sponded necessarily new directions of capitalist policy, reversing the old lines of free trade capitalism: the fight for monopoly all over the world, for exclusive areas of exploitation, markets, concessions; the division of the world between a handful of Great Powers, and an aggressive colonial policy; tariffs, subsidies and quotas; export of capital in close association with colonial policy; strengthening of the bureaucratic and military machine; advance to world war for the redivision of the world. For reformers to attack one or another aspect in isolation of these policies (tariffs, or armaments, or colonial policy, or war) without attacking monopoly capitalism itself, or to expect monopoly capitalism to pursue a different "more enlightened" policy, was like expecting a tiger to live on grass.

But monopoly capitalism means at the same time the *parasitic* stage of capitalism. The greater part of the world becomes tributary to the handful of great powers; the majority of mankind is paying tribute to a tiny group of financial oligarchies. The rentier class, living on dividends, and without any contact with production, develops in the imperialist countries; the numbers engaged in serving them develop; the proportion of those engaged in productive industry declines.

At the same time a proportion of the tribute of "superprofit" is used to buy off the upper strata of the working class in the imperialist countries, by concessions, social reform measures, corruption of labor leaders, etc. So develops the phenomenon of the "labor aristocracy" and "bourgeois labor parties" in the imperialist countries, whose leaders go hand in hand with the capitalists. This is the basis of opportunism or reformism in Europe and America, and the cause of the split in the working-class movement.

Monopoly capitalism, however, as its parasitic tendencies already reveal, is *dying* capitalism. Production has reached its maximum possible development under capitalism; its further development is now hindered and artifically restricted by the forms of capitalist monopoly. The productive forces are in conflict with the capitalist forms. The explosion of the World War violently demonstrates this. The time is ripe for the proletarian revolution.

3. THE CHIEF TASK OF OUR TIMES— THE WORLD REVOLUTION

In his pamphlet *The Chief Task of Our Times* (first published in *Isvestia,* March 14, 1918, and republished in pamphlet form) , Lenin wrote:

The human race is passing through great and difficult changes which have (one can say it without the least exaggeration) a world-liberating significance. The world is passing to the war of the oppressed against the oppressors. In this new war the oppressed are struggling for liberation from the yoke of capitalism; from the abyss of suffering, torment, hunger and brutalization; they desire to pass onward to the bright future of a communist society, to universal well-being and a secure peace.

And again:

Outside of socialism there is no deliverance of humanity from wars, from hunger, from the destruction of millions and millions of human beings.*

The center of Lenin's teaching was to make conscious that the world revolution was no longer a dream of the future, but was the direct, urgent, indispensable task of the present stage; that the objective conditions were already fully present in this final stage of "rotten-ripe" dying capitalism; that it was urgently essential for the subjective factor of the world proletariat to become

---

* "In Louis Blanc's Footsteps," *The Revolution of 1917,* Book I, pp. 111-114.

conscious of the situation and act; and that delay could only mean ever increasing "torment, hunger and brutalization," "the destruction of millions and millions of human beings." The two decades since 1914 have abundantly shown the truth of this, as the imperialist world, through delay of the revolution, advances through increasing crisis towards a new world war.

Lenin approached the problems and conception of the world revolution in an extremely living, concrete, realistic fashion. It was for him no dream of a millennium or sudden conquest of power to be achieved overnight in a few glorious battles by the international working class. It was, on the contrary, a whole epoch, extending probably over decades. Marx had already written in 1851 (in his *Revelations on the Communist Trial at Cologne*) :

We say to the workers: "You will have to go through fifteen, twenty, fifty years of civil wars and international wars, not only in order to change existing conditions, but also in order to change yourselves and fit yourselves for the exercise of political power."

In the same way Lenin wrote:

The transition from capitalism to socialism occupies an entire historical epoch. ("The Proletarian Revolution," Ch. III.)

More explicitly Lenin wrote:

The socialist revolution cannot take place in any other form than that of an epoch, uniting the civil war of the proletariat against the bourgeoisie in the leading countries with a whole series of democratic, revolutionary and national-emancipatory movements in the undeveloped, backward and oppressed countries. Why is this? It is because capitalism develops unequally. ("On a Caricature of Marxism and Imperialist Economism," 1916.)

Here Lenin brings out his key thought for the character and development of the world revolution. What

Marx had described in general terms of "fifteen, twenty, fifty years of civil wars and international wars," Lenin is able to describe in concrete terms, on the basis of his analysis of imperialism. The process of the world revolution is directly connected with the law of the unequal development of capitalism. In place of the old conception, common among the Second International distorters of Marxism, of a separate mechanical evolution of each country, as if in isolation, through the stages of capitalism and large-scale capitalism to socialism (leading to a constant bowing to capitalism in the name of "Marxism"), the world framework of capitalism is seen as a whole, with the bursting points of contradiction "the weakest links in the chain," where the revolution begins.

Imperialism has drawn the whole world closely into a single complex, no longer merely in the sense of the old bare uniformity of the world market, but in a whole series of stages of dependence and servitude, colonial countries, debtor countries, defeated countries, etc., reaching up in a pyramid to the final handful of financial oligarchies at the top, who are in turn at war among themselves and in constantly changing relations of strength. It is manifest that the struggle for liberation here can only be correctly understood as a single struggle and not in artificial compartments. All the contradictions of capitalism reach their highest point in the conditions of imperialism: first, the struggle of the proletariat against the bourgeoisie in the leading imperialist countries; second, the struggle of the colonial peoples for liberation from the imperialist yoke; third, the conflict of the imperialist powers among themselves; and fourth—in the post-War stage—the conflict of imperialism against the new rising workers' power, the Soviet Union. Through the combined development of all these conflicts the world revolution develops. "Imperialism," said Lenin, "is the eve of the socialist revolution."

Just as the proletariat in each country leads the struggle of all the exploited masses, so on the world scale the international proletariat leads the struggle of the colonial peoples for liberation from imperialism. It is the alliance of the proletariat in the leading imperialist countries and of the colonial masses fighting for liberation that is able to lead to the successful overthrow of imperialism. This develops as a process over many years, of separate struggles in different parts of the world, of imperialist wars and civil wars, of victories and defeats, to the growing extension of the base of the socialist revolution, and final victory of the world revolution.

4. THE DICTATORSHIP OF THE PROLETARIAT

If the center of Lenin's teaching is the understanding of the task of the world revolution as the urgent task of the present stage, the practical expression of this is the dictatorship of the proletariat.

Once again the theoretical formulation by Marx of the dictatorship of the proletariat as the necessary form of the transition to socialism, and as the essence of his revolutionary teachings, repeated by him in his writings from beginning to end, is brought to concrete realization and new living actuality by Lenin.

The teachings of Marx and Engels on the dictatorship of the proletariat became overlaid and forgotten after their death by the leaders of the Second International, who became soaked in bourgeois parliamentarism. Marx and Engels had taught the workers to use the forms of parliamentarism and universal suffrage solely

in order to organize the forces of the working class for
the inevitable final struggle, which could only take the
form of civil war. But the leaders of the Second International began to see the sham parliamentary forms as
the realities of power, and to preach the anti-Marxist
doctrine of the possibility of "pure democracy" within
capitalism and of the "conquest of power" by the proletariat through bourgeois parliaments. Where this
road of the so-called "democratic advance to socialism"
was to lead became fully demonstrated with the War
and after, when the leaders became completely united
with the capitalist state against the workers, and ended
finally in surrender to fascism.

Lenin revived the revolutionary Marxist teaching of
the dictatorship of the proletariat. He pricked the
bubble of bourgeois democracy. He reminded his
hearers of

the idea explained with the greatest scientific accuracy by
Marx and Engels, when they said that the democratic bourgeois republic was nothing but an apparatus for the oppression of the working class by the bourgeois class, of the
working masses by a handful of capitalists. ("Bourgeois
Democracy and the Dictatorship of the Proletariat," 1919.)

He wrote:

Bourgeois democracy, while constituting a great historical
advance in comparison with feudalism, nevertheless remains, and cannot but remain, a very limited, a very hypo-
critical institution, a paradise for the rich and a trap and a
delusion for the exploited and for the poor. (*The Proletarian Revolution,* Ch. II.)

In a thousand ways, with living examples from Britain,
France and the United States, he showed the hypocrisy
of the supposed "freedom" of the workers under bourgeois democracy, and the reality of the dictatorship of
the big capitalists.

The state, Marx had taught, is only "the executive committee of the ruling class." Under capitalism the state is the organ of the capitalist dicatorship. The only alternative is the dictatorship of the proletariat.

In capitalist society there can be no middle course between the capitalist dictatorship and proletarian dictatorship. Any dream of a third course is merely the reactionary lament of the lower middle class. ("Bourgeois Democracy and the Dictatorship of the Proletariat.")

The dictatorship of the proletariat is realized by the overthrow of the capitalist state machine, and the establishment of the working class as the ruling class through new organs of workers' rule—the Soviets or councils of workers' delegates. Thus is brought into being a new type of democracy, Soviet democracy or proletarian democracy—a thousand times more democratic, as Lenin constantly insisted, than bourgeois democracy, because for the first time drawing the masses directly into the work of administration and executive decision.

Lenin was not anti-democratic, as his enemies and some ignorant bourgeois admirers allege. On the contrary, it was because he was genuinely and profoundly democratic that he fought with such hatred the sham of bourgeois democracy, and fought for proletarian democracy as a very much higher democratic form, and as leading, through the abolition of classes, to the realization for the first time of the real and complete freedom and equality of classless society.

The dictatorship of the proletariat is a dictatorship of the immense majority against the minority of exploiters. It is the necessary weapon to carry through the class struggle to completion, to destroy the remains of the old order and build the new order.

The dictatorship of the proletariat is the fiercest, deepest cutting, most merciless war of the new class against the most powerful enemy, the bourgeoisie, whose power of resistance increases tenfold after its overthrow, even though overthrown in only one country. The power of the bourgeoisie rests not alone upon international capital, upon the strong international connections of this class, but also upon the *force of habit*, on the force of small industry, of which unfortunately there is plenty left, and which daily, hourly gives birth to capitalism and the bourgeoisie spontaneously and upon a large scale. Because of all this the dictatorship of the proletariat is indispensable. Victory over the bourgeoisie is impossible without a long, persistent, desperate life-and-death struggle, a struggle which requires constancy, discipline, firmness, inflexibility and concerted will-power.

And again:

The dictatorship of the proletariat is a resolute, persistent struggle against the forces and traditions of the old society; a struggle that is both bloody and non-bloody, both violent and peaceful, both military and economic, both educational and administrative.   (*"Left-Wing" Communism*, Ch. V.)

But the dictatorship of the proletariat is only a transitional form. As it completes its task, with the final ending of all forms of bourgeois resistance and the abolition of classes, the state as a machine of coercion disappears and gives place to communist society, or the equal participation of the masses in economic and social administration and cultural life.

The annihilation of the power of the state is the aim all Socialists have had in view, first and foremost amongst them, Marx. Without the realization of this aim, true democracy, that is, liberty and equality, is unattainable. It can only be achieved by the Soviet or proletarian democracy; for this system prepares at the very outset for the "withering away" of any form of state by bringing forward the mass organizations of the working people into a constant and absolute participation in state administration. ("Bourgeois Democracy and the Dictatorship of the Proletariat.")

5. NATIONAL AND COLONIAL LIBERATION

One of the most essential keys for the victory of the world revolution, as Lenin constantly insisted, is the union of the struggle of the proletariat in the leading imperialist countries and of the struggle for liberation of the oppressed nationalities and subject peoples in the colonial and semi-colonial countries.

In principle Marx had already made clear the importance of the question of national liberation for the working-class movement and for the world revolution, especially in his treatment of the Polish question and of the Irish question.

In the era of imperialism this question takes on a new and burning importance. The majority of mankind become reduced to colonial and semi-colonial subjection. Colonial exploitation becomes the main basis of strength of the bourgeoisie. The proletariat in the imperialist countries can only win emancipation in alliance with the struggle of the colonial peoples.

The leaders of the old Second International completely failed to understand the significance of this question. The official leadership passed resolutions in favor of "national freedom," "autonomy," etc., but always as within the framework of existing imperialist rule, and giving no practical support to the revolutionary struggle for independence. Another section argued that "national freedom" was only a bourgeois and not a socialist interest, and was therefore no concern of the working class; that socialism was opposed to the breaking up of larger economic units, etc. ("imperialist economism," as Lenin termed this latter argument). Both tendencies amounted in practice to support of imperialism.

Lenin first brought out the revolutionary significance of this question in the era of imperialism. Already before the war he gave close attention to the rising forces of struggle in Asia; in 1913 he wrote on "Backward Europe and Progressive Asia." During the War he worked out completely the analysis of every aspect of this question and showed the revolutionary significance of the slogan of "national self-determination." Against those who spoke of the Irish rebellion of 1916 as a *"putsch,"* he wrote:

To believe that a social revolution is possible without the revolt of the small nationalities and colonies in Europe, without the revolutionary outburst of the petty-bourgeoisie with all its prejudices, without a movement of the non-class conscious proletarian and semi-proletarian masses against landlord, clerical monarchist, national, etc., oppression—to believe this is tantamount to denying the social revolution altogether. . . .

Those who wait for a "pure" social revolution will never live to see it. Such a one is merely a revolutionary in words, without understanding the reality of revolution. ("The Results of the Discussion on Self-Determination," 1916.)

After the victory of the Soviet Revolution this question took on a still sharper significance. Lenin wrote:

While formerly prior to the epoch of world revolution movements for national liberation were a part of the general democratic movements, now, however, after the victory of the Soviet Revolution in Russia and the opening of the period of world revolution, the movement for national liberation is part of the world proletarian revolution.

At the Second Congress of the Communist International in 1920 he brought to the forefront the issue of the national and colonial struggle for liberation, and the necessity for the proletariat in the imperialist countries to give active support to it. The theses drafted by him declare:

The policy of the Communist International on national and colonial questions must be chiefly to bring about a union of the proletarian and working masses of all nations and countries for a joint revolutionary struggle leading to the overthrow of capitalism, without which national inequality and oppression cannot be abolished.

But the fight for the full right of separation of subject nations is no fight for separation as such, for fragmentation and petty-bourgeois nationalist conceptions of isolation. On the contrary, the right of full separation is only necessary in order to end all national oppression, and thus clear the way to the free union of all peoples. The goal remains world union, the ultimate "fusion of nations."

This demand is not at all equivalent to the demand for separation, fragmentation and establishment of petty states. It signifies only a logical expression of the struggle against every kind of national oppression. . . .

The goal of socialism is not only the destruction of the division of humanity into petty states and all kinds of individual nations, not merely the coming together of nations, but also their actual fusion. . . .

Just as humanity can only arrive at the destruction of classes through a transitional period of the dictatorship of the oppressed class, so also humanity can only arrive at the inevitable fusion of nations through a transitional period of the complete freedom of all oppressed nationalities, that is, their freedom of separation. ("The Socialist Revolution and the Right of Nations to Self-Determination," 1916.)

6. Tactics and Organization of the Revolution

In no sphere of Marxism did Lenin make a more distinctive or far-reaching contribution than in the very wide field of revolutionary strategy, tactics and organization. All these questions could still only receive incomplete treatment in the time of Marx, owing to the still early stage of development of the working-class movement. On the basis of the nineteenth century revolutions and of the first stages of development of the working-class movement to a mass basis, Marx was able to present in bold outline the essentials of revolutionary proletarian strategy and tactics; and the writings and correspondence of Marx and Engels in addition reveal a host of pregnant indications on a very great variety of specific questions. These indications, however, were in great part neglected, ignored or even opposed by their immediate successors, who took parts that suited them and often even suppressed the rest. Lenin, on the contrary, worked over anew these indications with the closest attention in the light of further experience, and at the same time faced with complete freshness the new problems of the more advanced stage of capitalism and the working-class movement. It was Lenin who first elaborated Marxist strategy and tactics into a fully worked out science.

This practical revolutionary science elaborated by Lenin, in close association with revolutionary theory, covers the whole range from the most elementary questions of agitation and organization to the ultimate questions of the conquest of power and of post-revolutionary construction. The mastery of dialectical method is here most powerfully exhibited, with the greatest elasticity in responding to each concrete situation, while maintaining the revolutionary line and aims unbroken. In consequence just this essence of Lenin's leadership least admits of any formal summarizing, and requires to be studied in the life.

At the center of Lenin's teaching on the tactics and organization of the revolution is the conception of the party, or conscious and organized vanguard of the working class. This conception reaches a development far more complete than was possible in the epoch of Marx. In the period of the proletarian revolution the workers' revolutionary party or Communist Party has to face enormously more developed tasks than in the preceding epoch. The party requires to be "the organized political lever by means of which the more advanced section of the working class leads the whole proletarian and semi-proletarian mass" ("Theses of the Second Congress of the Communist International"). The essence of the conception of the party is the conception of *leadership;* not leadership by a handful of individuals, but leadership by an organic section of the working class, the most conscious, revolutionary section, fighting in the front rank and leading the entire struggle, both before the revolution, during the revolution, and after the revolution. Without such leadership to unify and guide the struggle the forces of the workers are inevitably defeated by the highly organized and centralized forces of the bourgeoisie and of the bourgeois state. The working class, in order to conquer, requires to develop a Communist Party.

In order to be able to accomplish this task of leadership, the Communist Party requires to unite within its ranks all the most conscious, revolutionary, active, self-sacrificing workers; to be based on clear revolutionary theory with constant critical alertness to the situation; to be closely united with the mass of the workers and with all the exploited masses; to combine the strongest centralized discipline as a fighting organization with democracy in the election and control of higher organs and conscious participation of every member in the formulation and discussion of policy. This in turn requires corresponding forms of organization, the basing of the party primarily in the factories, the strongholds of the industrial working class, and in the mass organizations of the trade unions, etc.

All this conception marks a definite break with the old, loose type of parliamentary Social-Democratic parties common in the pre-War Second International. In the period after 1914 Lenin deliberately broke with

the name "Social-Democratic Party," which had always
been declared incorrect by Marx and Engels, and which
had now become identified with the traitor parties, and
brought into use again the original name used by Marx
and Engels and always declared by them to be alone
scientifically correct, the "Communist Party."

A long process of working-class struggle and experience, of partial battles, victories and retreats, of developing organization, of conflicts of tendencies, is necessary
before the working-class forces are strong and ready, and
before the mass Communist Party with effective leadership has developed out of the struggle, to be able to
advance at the favorable moment to the final overthrow
of bourgeois power. The leading Communist Party
adequate to its tasks does not come into being ready-
made from the moment of the formation of the first
nucleus towards such a party.

The proletarian revolutionary party does not deserve the
name until it learns to connect leaders, class, masses, into
one indissoluble whole. (*"Left-Wing" Communism,* Ch.
VI.)

The Communist Party is not the first, but the "last,
highest form of proletarian class organization." It
grows and develops with the growth and development
of the working-class struggle.

It is in this pre-revolutionary process of the marshal-
ing and organizing of the working-class forces, partial
preparatory battles, crystallizing of the revolutionary
advance-guard and winning of leadership in the working
class against the opportunist trends, that develop the
multifarious problems of tactics of the pre-revolutionary
period which Lenin worked out in close detail in the
experience of the Bolshevik Party up to 1917, and thereafter transmitted this experience through the Communist International to the working class in other
countries.

This experience and guidance covers a series of problems, centering round the relationship of the party to the masses, and the conquest of the majority of the working class: in particular, the rôle of the trade unions and the relation of the party to the trade unions and other mass organizations of the working class; the relation of the party to the semi-proletarian masses; the combination of legal and illegal activity; the utilization of bourgeois parliaments and elections, not for the purpose of spreading parliamentary illusions, but for the development of revolutionary working-class propaganda and organization; the rôle of partial struggles and demands, of reforms ("by-products of the revolutionary class struggle") , of retreats and maneuvers; the methods of the fight against opportunism, etc.

The great part of these tactical problems, which come to the front and are of decisive importance for advance in the pre-revolutionary period, continue and develop through new forms also in the revolutionary and post-revolutionary periods.

But still more far-reaching are the basic problems, strategical and tactical, of the leadership of the mass struggle as a whole up to the revolutionary situation and in the revolutionary situation itself, the determination of the whole line of advance, stage by stage, up to the final battle and the conquest of power. Here the task of leadership brings to the test the whole strength of Marxist-Leninist theory and practice: the correct estimation of the relation of class forces, of the internal and external situation, of the strength and stability of the bourgeoisie, of the degree of preparedness of the proletariat, of the rôle of the intermediate strata; the determination of the slogans and methods of struggle to mobilize the masses on the widest possible scale, and to win to the proletariat its reserves of support from other strata; the correct judgment of the revolutionary situa-

tion, when the old governing forces are discredited and
in break-up, and the masses are refusing to accept the
old conditions of life; the advance to increasingly radi-
cal transitional slogans and rising forms of struggle and
mass action; and the final decision of the moment for
the decisive battle, and direct leadership and organization of the insurrection.

Lastly, the leadership of Lenin after 1917 opens up
the hitherto completely untouched ground of the strategy and tactics of the proletarian leadership after the
conquest of power.

Three of the most famous statements of Lenin on
these fundamental questions of revolution may here be
given.

The first is his definition of a revolutionary situation:

The fundamental law of revolution, confirmed by all revolutions and particularly by the three Russian ones of the
twentieth century, is as follows. It is not sufficient for the
revolution that the exploited and oppressed masses understand the impossibility of living in the old way and demand
changes; for the revolution it is necessary that the exploiters
should not be able to rule as of old. Only when the masses
do not want the old régime, and when the rulers are *unable*
to govern as of old, then only can the revolution succeed.
This truth may be expressed in other words: revolution is
impossible without an all-national crisis, affecting both the
exploited and the exploiters. It follows that for the revolution it is essential, first, that a majority of the workers (or
at least a majority of the conscious, thinking, politically
active workers) should fully understand the necessity of a
revolution and be ready to sacrifice their lives for it; second,
that the ruling class be in a state of governmental crisis
which attracts even the most backward masses into politics
—a sign of every real revolution is the rapid, tenfold or even
hundredfold increase in the number of representatives of
the toiling and oppressed masses heretofore apathetic, representatives able to carry on the political fight which
weakens the government and facilitates its overthrow by the
revolutionists.   (*"Left-Wing" Communism.*)

To be successful, the uprising must be based not on a conspiracy, not on a party, but on the advanced class. This is the first point. The uprising must be based on the revolutionary upsurge of the people. This is the second point. The uprising must be based on the *crucial point* in the history of the maturing revolution, when the activity of the vanguard of the people is at its height, when the *vacillations* in the ranks of the enemies, and *in the ranks of the weak, half-hearted, undecided friends of the revolution are at their highest point*. This is the third point. It is in pointing out these three conditions as the way of approaching the question of an uprising, that Marxism differs from Blanquism.*

The third is his summary of the "art" of insurrection, drawing together the previous utterances of Marx and Engels on this question:

1. Never *play* at uprising, but once it is begun, remember firmly that you have to *go to the very end*.
2. It is necessary to gather *a great preponderance of forces* in a decisive place at a decisive moment, else the enemy, being in a position of better preparation and organization, will annihilate the insurgents.
3. Once the uprising has been begun, one must act with the greatest decisiveness, one must take the offensive, absolutely, and under all circumstances. "Defense is the death of an armed uprising."
4. One must strive to take the enemy by surprise, to take advantage of a moment when his troops are scattered.
5. One must try *daily* for at least small successes (one may even say hourly, when it is a question of one city), thus maintaining under all circumstances a "moral superiority." **

These examples are typical of the concrete, living, simultaneously theoretical and practical approach of Lenin to the fundamental problems of revolution.

The leadership of Lenin ranges over the whole de-

* "Marxism and Uprising," in *Toward the Seizure of Power*, Book I, pp. 224-229.
** "Advice from an Outsider," in *Toward the Seizure of Power*, Book II, pp. 97-99.

velopment of the working-class struggle from the earliest stages to the direct advance in a revolutionary situation to the conquest of power, and to the tasks beyond the conquest of power.

In all these fields of the working-class struggle, from the earliest stages to beyond the conquest of power, Lenin leaves a legacy of leadership, of theoretical and practical guidance, the absorption of which by the international working class opens the way to victory.

This leadership receives its organized embodiment and collective form in the Communist International, founded under the leadership of Lenin in 1919, as the union of the revolutionary working class, on the basis of the principles of Marxism and Leninism, for the victory of the world socialist revolution.

CHAPTER IV

THE HEIR OF LENIN—THE COMMUNIST INTERNATIONAL

NINETEEN THIRTY-FOUR witnesses the tenth anniversary of the death of Lenin.

How far have these ten years confirmed the correctness of his line and his outlook?

These ten years have seen the collapse of all the capitalist dreams of "recovery" after the War, the increasing breakdown of the Versailles settlements, the advance of imperialism to still more intense conflicts, the development for over four years now of a world economic crisis without parallel in intensity and duration, and the ever more universally recognized approach to a new world war.

These same ten years have seen the advance of the Soviet Union from the weakness and economic paralysis consequent on war and civil war to heights of economic construction without parallel in their tempo and extent in the history of capitalism; to a level of production multiplied more than fourfold in a decade and over three times pre-War, alongside actual decline at the some time in every capitalist country, and already bringing the Soviet Union to the rank of the second greatest industrial country in the world, with Britain falling to third place and Germany to fourth. Whatever the future battles that still await the Soviet Union and the world revolution, these achievements, and still more the profound cultural work that has been achieved, can never be destroyed, and constitute already the first foundation of the future world order.

Finally, these ten years have seen the advance and

intensification of the class struggle; the development of the process of revolutionization, not only in Europe and America, but also throughout Asia; the increasing breakdown of the forms of bourgeois democracy in the growing intensity of the struggle; the new collapse and surrender of the Second International to fascism; and the use of the most desperate methods and last resources of violent counter-revolution and fascism to maintain the decaying power of capitalism.

Lenin was not able to live to see these ten years of realization of all that he had indicated, of rapid unfolding of the decline of capitalism and of the advance of the world revolution. He was not able to give his direct leadership to the world in these most critical years of the world situation, when his leadership has been most sharply needed.

But he left behind him the forces and the organized forms to carry on the fight.

It was an essential characteristic of Lenin that from the beginning to the end of his political life he acted, never as an individual leader, but always as the conscious and responsible representative of a movement greater than any individual, which existed before he was born, and which continues after he is dead.

That movement of the international working class, of the international socialist revolution, which found its first forms nearly a century ago in the Communist League of Marx and Engels, which developed through the First International under the leadership of Marx and Engels, and through the forms of the pre-War Second International, he carried forward to a new stage and to new heights in the period of the proletarian revolution, through the forms of the Communist International.

The Communist International is the heir of Lenin.

In 1901 Kautsky, then the recognized theoretical leader of international socialism, wrote:

The revolutionary center is moving from the West to the East. In the first half of the nineteenth century this center was in France, some time in England. In 1848 Germany entered the ranks of revolutionary nations. The new century is being ushered in by such events as induce us to think that we are confronted by a further removal of the revolutionary center, namely, to Russia. Russia, which has imbibed so much revolutionary initiative from the West, is now perhaps itself ready to serve as a source of revolutionary energy. The Russian revolutionary movement which is now bursting into flame will perhaps become the strongest means for the extermination of the senile philistinism and sedate politics which is beginning to spread in our ranks, and will again rekindle the militant spirit and the passionate devotion to our great ideals.

Russia has long ceased to be for western Europe a prop for reaction and absolutism. The case now may be said to be reversed. . . . However the present struggle in Russia may end, the blood of the martyrs who have originated from it, unfortunately in too great numbers, will not have been shed in vain. It will nourish the shoots of the socialist revolution throughout the civilized world and make them flourish more quickly. In 1848 the Slavs were that crackling frost which killed the flowers of spring of the awakening peoples; perhaps now they are destined to be that storm which will break through the ice of reaction and will irresistibly bring with it the new happy spring of the peoples. (Kautsky, *The Slavs and the Revolution*, 1901, quoted by Lenin in *"Left-Wing" Communism*, Ch. I.)

We are witnessing the realization of this in very much more far-reaching forms than could have been foreseen at the time.

The Bolshevik Revolution of 1917 opened a new world era, the era of the world socialist revolution. For this reason, its significance is not primarily Russian, but international. The leadership of Lenin is not primarily Russian, but an international leadership.

The expression of this international leadership is the Communist International.

The conception of the Communist International or Third International was reached by Lenin already in 1914, immediately following the collapse of the Second International. At that time he wrote of its task in contrast to that of the Second International:

The Second International did its full share of useful preparatory work in the preliminary organization of the proletarian masses during the long "peaceful" epoch of the most cruel capitalist slavery and most rapid capitalist progress in the last third of the nineteenth and in the beginning of the twentieth century. The Third International is confronted with the task of organizing the forces of the proletariat for a revolutionary onslaught on the capitalist governments, for civil war against the bourgeoisie of all countries, for political power, for the victory of Socialism.*

The Communist International was founded in 1919. In its first three Congresses, from 1919 to 1921, Lenin took closest part and led the entire work, both in respect of organization, formulation of policy and the drafting of the principal documents. In the Fourth Congress in 1922 he still took part, although he was only able to do so to a limited extent.

Lenin was under no illusions as to the heavy task confronting the Communist International, or the long and painful process necessary before reaching the strength for victory. In August, 1921, after the Third Congress, he wrote:

We have now a Communist army throughout the whole world; though as yet poorly developed and badly organized. To forget or seek to conceal this fact would be merely to endanger the cause. It is our duty to build up and organize this army, to train it in all sorts of movements and struggles, in attacks and retreats, in which great care should be observed in studying the experiences of each movement.

* V. I. Lenin, *The Imperialist War*, p. 89.

There can be no victory apart from this tedious and hard schooling. ("Letter to the German Communist Party," October, 1921.)

Lenin knew that a long process of struggle was in front, with inevitably many defeats, and temporary victories of the counter-revolution in particular countries.

The bourgeoisie sees in Bolshevism only one side . . . insurrection, violence, terror; it endeavors, therefore, to prepare itself, especially for resistance and opposition in that direction alone. It is possible that in single cases, in single countries, for more or less short periods, they will succeed. We must reckon with such a possibility, and there is absolutely nothing dreadful to us in the fact that the bourgeoisie might succeed in this. Communism "springs up" from positively all sides of social life, its sprouts are everywhere, without exception—the "contagion" (to use the favorite and "pleasantest" comparison of the bourgeoisie and the bourgeois police) has very thoroughly penetrated into the organism and has totally impregnated it. If one of the "vents" were to be stopped up with special care, "contagion" would find another, sometimes most unexpected vent. Life will assert itself. Let the bourgeoisie rave, let it work itself into a frenzy, commit stupidities, take vengeance in advance on the Bolsheviks and endeavor to exterminate in India, Hungary, Germany, etc., more hundreds, thousands, and hundreds of thousand of the Bolsheviks of yesterday or those of to-morrow. Acting thus, the bourgeoisie acts as did all classes condemned to death by history. The Communists must know that the future at any rate is theirs; therefore we can and must unite the intensest passion in the great revolutionary struggle with the coolest and soberest calculations of the mad ravings of the bourgeoisie. . . . In all cases and in all countries Communism grows: its roots are so deep that persecution neither weakens nor debilitates, but rather strengthens it (*"Left-Wing" Communism*, Ch. X.)

"Life will assert itself." In this basic understanding Lenin proclaimed his confidence in the final victory of the world socialist revolution, despite all reverses and temporary defeats, exemplified to-day in the temporary rule of fascism in Germany, which can only pave the way for a new and deeper and finally victorious revolutionary upheaval.

Only the proletarian, socialist revolution is able to lead humanity out of the blind alley created by imperialism and imperialist wars. Whatever difficulties, possible temporary reverses, and waves of counter-revolution the revolution may encounter, the final victory of the proletariat is certain.*

Through the Communist International it falls to those living after Lenin, in conditions of deepening world crisis and urgency, to be able to carry forward this fight, a fight for no limited aims, but for a new era of humanity, to the final victory, which it was his triumph to inaugurate, but which he could not live to complete.

* "Materials Relating to the Revision of the Party Program," *The Revolution of 1917*, Book I, p. 327.

BIBLIOGRAPHY

NOTES ON BOOKS FOR ENGLISH READERS

I. WRITINGS OF LENIN

(1) COLLECTED WORKS.—The complete collected edition of Lenin's writings is still only available in Russian. It is in process of issue, however, in German, French and English. The only authorized English translation is issued by International Publishers and is based on the revised and edited texts prepared by the Marx-Engels-Lenin Institute. Each volume is provided with biographical, bibliographical and extensive explanatory notes and contains important related documents to assist the reader. The following volumes have already appeared:

The Iskra Period (2 volumes). Covers the formative period of the Bolshevik Party.

Materialism and Empirio-Criticism. A critique of attempted revisions of the philosophic base of Marxism and an exposition of dialectic materialism.

The Imperialist War. An analysis of the causes of the World War and the formulation of Bolshevik policy with regard to it.

The Revolution of 1917 (2 volumes). From the overthrow of the Tsar to the first open conflict with the Kerensky Government in July, 1917.

Towards the Seizure of Power (2 volumes). From the July Days to the Bolshevik Revolution of November, 1917.

A shortened *Selected Works* is also in preparation, to be completed in six books, comprising 12 volumes, in which Lenin's writings will be arranged topically.

(2) SEPARATE WORKS.—The most important separate works available so far in English and issued by International Publishers are:

What Is To Be Done? (1902)
The Teachings of Karl Marx (1914)
Socialism and War (1915)
The Collapse of the Second International (1915), issued under the title "The War and the Second International."
Imperialism, the Highest Stage of Capitalism (1916)
State and Revolution (1917)
"Left-Wing" Communism: An Infantile Disorder (1920)
Letter to the American Workers (1918)

The following special works or collections of articles and speeches on the Russian Revolution of 1917:

Letters from Afar
The Tasks of the Proletariat in Our Revolution
The April Conference
The Threatening Catastrophe and How to Fight It
Will the Bolsheviks Maintain State Power?
On the Eve of October

(3) SELECTIONS AND EXTRACTS
Lenin on Britain
The Paris Commune
The Revolution of 1905
Religion
Lenin on the Jewish Question
Speeches of Lenin

II. LIFE OF LENIN

Memoirs made available by International Publishers include:
N. K. Krupskaya, *Memories of Lenin.* Vol. 1, 1894-1907; Vol. II, 1908-1917.
Clara Zetkin: *Reminiscences of Lenin.*
Maxim Gorky: *Days With Lenin.*
A life of Lenin for boys and girls: *Our Lenin,* by Ruth Shaw and Harry Alan Potamkin, drawings by William Siegel.

III. LENINISM

The standard work is:
Joseph Stalin: *Leninism* (2 volumes). Volume I contains *"Problems of Leninism"* and *"Foundations of Leninism"* (which have also been issued separately under the same titles); Volume II contains Stalin's major speeches and writings dealing with the application of Leninism to present problems.
Joseph Stalin: *Lenin*

IV. THE WRITINGS OF MARX AND ENGELS.—Fundamental to an understanding of Leninism are the basic works of Marx and Engels of which International Publishers have already issued, in new translations and extensively annotated:

Manifesto of the Communist Party
Wage-Labour and Capital
The Civil War in France
Germany: Revolution and Counter-Revolution
Critique of the Gotha Programme
The Peasant War in Germany
The Eighteenth Brumaire of Louis Bonaparte
Class Struggles in France
Letters to Kugelmann
Ludwig Feuerbach
Anti-Dühring

Other basic works are now being prepared with the aid of the Marx-Engels-Lenin Institute.

V. ADVICE TO READERS

The reader who is completely a beginner without previous acquaintance with the subject-matter, and who wishes to make an elementary study of Lenin and Leninism, may be recommended:

(1) First to acquaint himself with the general conceptions of Marxism through Lenin, *The Teachings of Karl Marx;*

(2) then to read some of the most important writings of Lenin, especially *State and Revolution, Imperialism, "Left-Wing" Communism;*

(3) then to acquaint himself further with the Russian Revolution through such books as John Reed, *Ten Days That Shook the*

World and the *Illustrated History of the Russian Revolution* (International Publishers), reading alongside some of Lenin's 1917 writings;

(4) to read some fuller Life such as Krupskaya's *Memories of Lenin;*

(5) to extend his understanding of Leninism by acquainting himself with *The Programme of the Communist International* and Stalin's *Foundations of Leninism.*

Thereafter the reader can extend his reading according to interest in all the available writings of Lenin, best of all, through the *Collected Works,* which has invaluable full explanatory matter to assist the reader.

The most important is to read Lenin's own writings, which (with rare exceptions) are not difficult, but written in an extremely clear, lively, forceful style. It is, however, useless to skim them; they require to be read with close attention and active thought, since the argument is packed with extreme economy.

The student, if he is to understand Leninism, should not treat it as a historical study, but requires to maintain close contact with the current literature of the living movement of Marxism-Leninism (*Communist International, International Press Correspondence, The Communist, Daily Worker*).